MYSTERIES OF THE VIRGIN MARY

MYSTERIES OF THE VIRGIN MARY

Living Our Lady's Graces

FR. PETER JOHN CAMERON, O.P.

SERVANT
BOOKS

PUBLISHED BY ST. ANTHONY MESSENGER PRESS
CINCINNATI, OHIO

Grateful acknowledgment is made to the following for permission to reprint previously published material: Abbey Press, *Virgin Wholly Marvelous: Praises of Our Lady by the Popes, Councils, Saints, and Doctors of the Church*, ©1981, by David Supple, ed.; Alba House, *Fifteen Mysteries in the Life of Jesus*, ©2002, by Richard Hobbs; Alleluia Press, *Byzantine Daily Worship*, ©1969; Catholic Book Publishing, *Prayers to Mary*, ©1987, by Virgilio Noe, ed.; Dedalus Press, *The Life of the Virgin Mary: A Cycle of Poems*, ©2003, by Rainer Maria Rilke, Christine McNeill, trans.; Ignatius Press, *Mary and the Fathers of the Church: The Blessed Virgin Mary in Patristic Thought*, ©1999, by Luigi Gambero, Thomas Buffer, trans., and *Mary in the Middle Ages: The Blessed Virgin Mary in the Thought of the Medieval Latin Theologians*, ©2000, by Luigi Gambero, Thomas Buffer, trans.; Libreria Editrice Vaticana, *Theotokos: Woman, Mother, Disciple: A Catechesis on Mary*, ©2000, by Pope John Paul II and *On the Most Holy Rosary (Rosarium Virginis Mariae): Apostolic Letter on the Most Holy Rosary*, ©2002, by Pope John Paul II; Paulist Press, *Sor Juana Inés de la Cruz: Selected Writings*, ©2005, by Pamela Kirk Rappaport, trans.; Rowman & Littlefield, *Mexican Spirituality: Its Sources and Mission in the Earliest Guadalupan Sermons*, ©2002, by Francisco Raymond Schulte; and TAN Books, *The Wonder of Guadalupe: The Origin and Cult of the Miraculous Image of the Blessed Virgin in Mexico*, ©1981. Every effort has been made to trace copyright holders. If there is any error or omission, the publishers will be happy to correct this at the first opportunity.

Unless otherwise noted, Scripture passages have been taken from the *Revised Standard Version*, Catholic edition. Copyright 1946, 1952, 1971 by the Division of Christian Education of the National Council of Churches of Christ in the USA. Used by permission. All rights reserved.

Scripture texts marked *NAB* are taken from the *New American Bible*. Copyright 1970, Confraternity of Christian Doctrine.

Note: The editors of this volume have made minor changes in capitalization to some of the Scripture quotations herein. Please consult the original source for proper capitalization.

Quotes are taken from the English translation of the *Catechism of the Catholic Church* for the United States of America (indicated as *CCC*), 2nd ed. Copyright 1997 by United States Catholic Conference—Libreria Editrice Vaticana.

Cover and book design by Mark Sullivan
Cover image: Gerard David (c.1450-1523) *Virgin and Child with Four Angels*.
Cover image copyright © The Metropolitan Museum of Art / Art Resource, NY

LIBRARY OF CONGRESS CATALOGING-IN-PUBLICATION DATA
Cameron, Peter John.
Mysteries of the Virgin Mary : living Our Lady's graces / Peter John Cameron.
p. cm.
Includes bibliographical references (p.   ) and index.
ISBN 978-0-86716-925-6 (pbk. : alk. paper)
1. Mary, Blessed Virgin, Saint. I. Title.
BT603.C36 2010
232.91—dc22
2010013535

ISBN 978-0-86716-925-6

Published by Servant Books, an imprint of St. Anthony Messenger Press.
28 W. Liberty St.
Cincinnati, OH 45202
www.AmericanCatholic.org
www.ServantBooks.org

Printed in the United States of America.

Printed on acid-free paper.

11 12 13 14 5 4 3 2

For my mother
who loves the Blessed Mother

Mary does bring us closer to Christ; she does lead us to him,
provided that we live her mystery in Christ.

—Pope John Paul II
Gift and Mystery

contents

preface

S<small>T.</small> T<small>HÉRÈSE</small> <small>OF</small> L<small>ISIEUX</small>, <small>DOCTOR</small> <small>OF</small> <small>THE</small> C<small>HURCH</small>, once said, "For a sermon on the Blessed Virgin to please me and do me any good, I must see her real life, not her imagined life. [Preachers] should present her as imitable, bringing out her virtues, saying that she lived by faith just like ourselves."[1]

The aim of this book is to present the "real life" of the Blessed Virgin Mary as it is commemorated in the Marian liturgical feasts of the Church. The *Catechism of the Catholic Church* teaches that "'the Church's devotion to the Blessed Virgin is intrinsic to Christian worship.' The Church rightly honors 'the Blessed Virgin with special devotion.'... The liturgical feasts dedicated to the Mother of God...express this devotion to the Virgin Mary" (*CCC*, 971, quoting Pope Paul VI, *Marialis Cultus*, 56).

We may well wonder, why does the Church venerate the Blessed Virgin Mary according to these particular liturgical feasts drawn from her life? And what do the mysteries of Mary's life have to do concretely with our own? These are the questions that this book seeks to address.

Much of the confusion and dissatisfaction and sadness we experience day to day come from our own struggles with "real life." We need someone to help us look at our life, to show us who we are, to help us become ourselves and live fully. That is why we turn with devotion to the real life of the Mother of God. In seeing how Mary lived by faith, we can find the courage and grace to do the same, united with her.

The Blessed Virgin Mary brings us closer to Christ as we live her mystery in Christ. When we talk about "mystery," we mean something that we acknowledge—that we recognize to be real and true—but that we do not possess. When we say "mystery" we speak of an Other who changes us. We long for that transforming change to take hold of us.

Yet, as St. Thomas Aquinas observes, "sublime mysteries should not be explained to everyone immediately, but should be handed down through superiors to others in their proper turn."[2] And so we willingly confide ourselves to God's mother, celebrating sacramentally the mysteries of the Blessed Virgin Mary, so as to be in communion with Our Lady in the way that she continues to live her mystery in Christ.

With this end in mind, this book endeavors to offer spiritual perspectives on the Blessed Virgin Mary's life that are ordered to aiding meditation on the Marian mysteries. Key to this is the inclusion of the insights of many mystics and spiritual masters regarding the Blessed Virgin Mary (including a number of voices new to me).

This book can be read from beginning to end, and then picked up again on each Marian feast throughout the Church's liturgical year. While it is intended for everyone, my hope is that priests and deacons who preach the mysteries of the Blessed Virgin Mary will find this little book beneficial.

In a special way I owe my devotion to the Blessed Virgin Mary to Father Romanus Cessario, O.P., whose exemplary love for Our Lady moved me to ask him to teach me about the Mother of God and her instrumental role in the life of faith. I am deeply thankful to Father Cessario for his witness, his instruction, and his friendship.

I would like to thank my acquisitions editor, Cynthia Cavnar, who came up with the idea for this book and asked me to write it. I am especially grateful for the clerical assistance of Catherine Kolpak, a most ardent devotee of the Blessed Mother.

May all who read this book be blessed to discover how God intends Our Lady's graces for our lives.

—Father Peter John Cameron, O.P.
St. Mary Priory, New Haven, Connecticut
Solemnity of the Immaculate Conception
December 8, 2009

chapter one

WHY PRAY TO MARY?
Seven Reasons for Marian Devotion

POPE JOHN PAUL II MADE THE CLAIM THAT "IT IS impossible to proclaim Jesus Christ, true God and true man, without referring to the Virgin Mary, his Mother."[1] That "reference" is what we call Marian devotion. Why is it crucial to living the faith?

One: God Has Marian Devotion

We hear the ardor of God's heart expressed in the book of Hosea:

> I will allure her…
>   and speak to her heart.…
>
> I will espouse you to me forever;
>   I will espouse you in right and in justice,
>   in love and in mercy;

I will espouse you in fidelity,

and you shall know the LORD.

(Hosea 2:16, 21–22, *NAB*)

This age-old longing, this promise, comes to fruition finally when God, through the angelic messenger, speaks words of espousal to the Blessed Virgin Mary at the Annunciation: "Hail, full of grace, the Lord is with you!" (Luke 1:28). As the great master of Marian devotion St. Louis-Marie de Montfort (+1716) explains, "The Hail Mary…is the most perfect compliment you can offer to Mary, because it is the compliment which the Most High God Himself made to her, through an Archangel, in order to win her heart."[2]

The motivation behind our affection is identical to that of God: "We do not love the Blessed Virgin specifically because of what we obtain, or hope to obtain, from her; but we love her because she is worthy of our love."[3] In fact, God's heart is so given over in love for Mary that we would miss out on something of God's love if we did not share his predilection for her. As Louis de Montfort expresses it: "I do not believe that any person can achieve intimate union with Our Lord…unless he has established a very deep union with the Blessed Virgin and a great dependence on her help."[4]

Accordingly, "all who take delight in God should take delight in Mary, and in the delight that he has in her and she in him,"[5] wrote Bl. Julian of Norwich (+1416). And St. Peter Chrysologus (+450) claimed, "He who is not awestruck by this Virgin's spirit and who does not admire her soul is ignorant of how great God is."[6] Put even more exuberantly by St. Methodius (+311), "You, O great Mother, are the beginning, the middle and the end of our happiness."[7]

Two: Christ Commands Us to Behold Our Mother

The best reason for practicing Marian devotion is obedience. Our Lord Jesus Christ from the cross commanded, "Behold, your mother!" (John 19:27). The need to esteem Mary as our Mother is a tenet of revelation. Thus St. Bernard of Clairvaux (+1153) exhorts us, "Let us venerate Mary with every fiber of our being, from the deepest part of our heart, because this is the will of him who wanted us to receive everything through Mary."[8] St. Louis de Montfort echoes this: "It is the most decided wish of her Son that we should come to him through his Blessed Mother."[9]

Jesus spent every instant of his ministry giving us exactly what we needed to overcome our resistance to God so as to live predisposed to the happiness that is our destiny. The supreme gift of self that Christ unfailingly offered to men and women did not end at the hour of his death; on the contrary, it was *intensified and perfected*. Christ reserved his best, his most powerful and most effective gifts, for the end: the gift of himself in the Eucharist and the gift of his Blessed Mother. And since Christ's whole earthly life was revelation of the Father (see *CCC*, 516), the handing over of Mary as our mother constitutes a preordained way for us to come to know the Father. This inspired St. Ildephonsus (+667) to pray, "In order to be a devoted servant of the Father, I faithfully desire to be the servant of the Mother."[10]

Who but the Immaculate Mother of God knows how to love Jesus Christ as he deserves? Christ gives us Mary to be our mother so that we might pray with St. Anselm of Canterbury (+1109): "O good Mother, I pray you for the love with which you love your Son, that you might grant me to love him truly as you truly love him and as you wish him to be loved."[11]

As far as our "beholding" goes, the young Jesuit St. John Berchmans (+1621) assures us that "any devotion, however small, will please Mary, provided it be constant."[12] Origen reminds us how indispensable devotion to Mary is for our salvation: "The profound meaning [of the Gospel of John] cannot be perceived except by him who rested his head on Jesus' breast and who received Mary to be his mother also."[13]

Three: All God Does in Mary He Does for Us

We may be tempted to balk at Mary's perfections. Reflecting on her goodness and virtues can remind us of our own depressing defects and failings. We might even feel alienated by her glories because Our Lady seems so unlike us in our fallenness and misery.

A help for this aversion comes in a revelation the Lord made to Bl. Julian of Norwich: "It is for love of you that I have made Mary so exalted, so noble, so honorable; and this delights me. And I wish it to delight you."[14] Every grace that God has given to Mary he has given to her for us. The blessings bestowed upon Our Lady are bound to be ours.

Again and again St. Louis de Montfort returns to a cardinal point: "The Blessed Virgin is the means used by Christ to come to us; and she is also the means we must use to go to Him.... Her master purpose is to unite us with Jesus Christ her Son."[15]

God intends the excellence with which he imbued the Virgin Mary to be a cause of hope for us. The radiance we experience in her erases our resistance. The saints join their voices in affirming that the practice of Marian devotion stands as a sure indication of a person's predestination:

St. John of Avila (+1569) states, "It is one of the signs of those who are to be saved to have a great devotion to Mary."[16]

The eighth-century St. John of Damascus prays: "To be devout towards you, O Holy Virgin, is a weapon of salvation that God gives to those whom He wills to save."[17]

And God pledges through St. Catherine of Siena (+1380): "My goodness has decreed that anyone at all, just or sinner, who holds Mary in due reverence will never be snatched or devoured by the infernal demon."[18]

Four: Our Lady Is Our Principle of Purity Before God

If we are honest we will admit that we do not possess the right, the innate worthiness, to stand before God as his equal. If we require a letter of recommendation to get a job or to go to college, why shouldn't it be so with God?

Here, too, St. Louis de Montfort aids our understanding. He asks, "Is our purity sufficiently great to warrant our uniting ourselves with [God], directly and of ourselves?"[19] Clearly the answer is no. Rather, "it is Mary alone who has found grace before God without the aid of another mere creature. All others who have found grace with God have done so only through her, and this will be true also of all who at any time become pleasing to God."[20] Mary the Immaculate Conception is so "wholly united with God and, as it were, lost in God," says de Montfort, that "there never has been, nor ever shall be, a creature who assists us more efficaciously in achieving" perfection through union with God.[21]

De Montfort continues his good instruction:

Man—so corrupt—so weak and so inconstant—trusts in himself, relies on his own strength, and believes himself capable of preserving intact the treasury of his own graces, virtues and merits. Now, by this devotion, we give into the safe keeping of the Blessed Virgin all that we possess.... We trust in her fidelity; we lean on her strength; we build upon her mercy and her charity, in order that she may preserve and increase our virtues and our merits, despite all the efforts of the world, the flesh, and the devil, to deprive us of them.[22]

Relying on the Blessed Mother as our principle of purity before God garners untold graces. The Cistercian St. Amadeus of Lausanne (+1159) asks: "Who did ever come away from her company sick or downcast, or devoid of some knowledge of the heavenly mysteries? ... Who did ever return home bereft of joy, after having entreated Mary, Mother of God, in behalf of his needs?"[23]

Five: God Wills to Give Us His Graces Through the Blessed Virgin Mary

To rescue us from the ever-present threat of self-reliance and self-contentment so dominant in us as a result of original sin, God gives us Mary to be the "dispenser" of graces. The age-old chorus of accord on this point is awesome:

> *St. Ildephonsus:* "O Mary, God has decided on committing all good gifts that He has provided for people to your hands, and therefore He has entrusted all treasures and riches of grace to you."[24]
>
> *St. Germanus of Constantinople (+730):* "No one, O you

Most Pure One, receives God's gifts but through your hands. No one, O you Most Worthy of Honor, is given grace by the Divine Mercy but by you."[25]

St. Peter Damian (+1072): "In your hands, O Mary, are the riches of the Divine mercies."[26]

St. Bernard of Clairvaux: "Seeing that we are unworthy to receive God's graces immediately from his hand, God gives them to Mary, in order that through her we may receive all that He wishes to give us."[27]

St. Thomas Aquinas (+1274): "The Virgin is called full of grace because she distributes this Divine life to all."[28]

St. Bridget of Sweden (+1373): "There is no one who prays that does not receive graces through the charity of the Virgin."[29]

St. Antoninus (+1459): "All graces that have ever been bestowed…, all came through Mary."[30]

St. Lawrence of Brindisi (+1619): "Every gift, every grace, every good that we have and that we receive continually, we receive through Mary."[31]

St. John Eudes (+1680): "[God's] divine goodness never has given and never will give any grace to anybody but through the hands and the Heart of her who is the Treasurer and Almoner of all His gifts."[32]

St. Alphonsus Liguori (+1787): "Mary is the mediatress of grace; … whatever graces we receive, they come to us through her intercession."[33]

St. Louis de Montfort explains the logic of this: "It was through Mary alone that God the Father gave His only-begotten Son to the world…. The world was unworthy, says Saint Augustine, to receive the Son of God immediately from the hands of the Father: He gave that Son to Mary, in order that the world should receive Him through her."[34] Thus, by divine design,

> it is through [Mary] that [the Son of God] applies His merits to His members, communicates to them His virtues and distributes to them His graces.... [S]he distributes to whom she wishes, as she wishes and when she wishes, all His gifts and graces, He Himself making no heavenly gift to [people] except by her virginal hands.[35]

The wisdom of this decision appears in the transformed humanity we gain as a fruit of it. St. John of Avila comments on this change: "If you are devoted to [Mary], you will feel temptations melting away, like wax before the fire."[36] Bl. Aelred of Rievaulx (+1166) attests: "By means of the Virgin's fullness of grace, the elements of the world are renewed, the infernal regions are destroyed, and the heavenly regions are restored; men are set free, and demons are trampled underfoot."[37] Put simply by Louis de Montfort, "In Mary and through Mary, God the Holy Spirit wills to form his elect."[38]

Six: Devotion to Mary Increases Our Intimacy With Christ

One (unfounded) rationalization for eschewing devotion to the Blessed Virgin Mary is that it somehow "interferes" with our relationship with Christ. But just the opposite is true. Once again we turn to St. Louis de Montfort, with his almost mathematical logic, to guide us.

The Blessed Virgin Mary, St. Louis tells us, is the creature who is most conformed to Jesus Christ. Since this is so, "the more we are consecrated to Mary, the more perfectly are we united with

Jesus Christ."[39] He reasons this way:

> The Inaccessible drew near to us, and united Himself
> closely, perfectly and even personally with our humanity,
> through Mary, without any detriment to His Divine
> Majesty; and it is also through Mary that we can draw
> near to God and unite ourselves perfectly and closely to
> His Divine Majesty, without fear of being repulsed.[40]

Thus the aim of true devotion to the most Blessed Virgin "is
none other than to establish more perfectly the worship of Jesus
Christ, and to provide an easier and safer way by which we can
find Jesus Christ."[41] "[D]evotion to the Blessed Virgin," St.
Louis insists, "is a *secure* way of reaching Jesus Christ and of
acquiring perfection through uniting ourselves with him."[42]
Conversely, he holds that "one of the reasons why Jesus Christ
is not known as he deserves to be known" is because "Mary has
been but very imperfectly known until now."[43] In sum, "whoever desires to have the fruit of life, Jesus Christ, must have the
tree of life, which is Mary."[44]

We need only look at how God acts in history to verify this.
The renowned seventeenth-century preacher Bishop Jacques-
Bénigne Bossuet wrote: "Christ has honored [Mary] by annihi-
lating and subjecting himself in her, and by communicating with
man through her."[45] And Christ continues to communicate and
offer communion to us through her. The medieval French theologian and poet Alain de Lille (+1202) well noted: "Without the
faith of the glorious Virgin, someone seeking Christ would be
able to wander but unable to make any progress."[46] But "whoever
finds Mary shall find life—that is, shall find Jesus Christ."[47]

Pope John Paul II emphatically took up this theme:

> Mary is the way which leads to Christ, and that filial
> devotion to her takes nothing from intimacy with Jesus.
> Indeed, it increases it and leads to the highest levels of
> perfection.... By looking at Mary, the believer learns to
> live in deeper communion with Christ, to adhere to him
> with a living faith and to place his trust and his hope in
> him, loving him with his whole being.[48]

In his zeal to drive home this point, Louis de Montfort proposes
the analogy of Mary as a mold: "Mary is the great and unique
mold of God, designed to create living images of God at little cost
and in but a short time; ... a person who has discovered this
mold, and who loses himself in it, is quickly transformed in Jesus
Christ, of Whom this mold is the true reproduction."[49]

Seven: We Are Devoted to Mary Because She Is Devoted to Us

From the cross Jesus commands the Beloved Disciple, "Behold,
your mother!" But first he says to Mary, "Woman, behold, your
son!" (John 19:26–27). And she does. "Mary not only comes to us
when called," says St. Jerome, "but even spontaneously advances
to meet us."[50]

Unbidden the Blessed Virgin set out for the hill country of
Judah to visit her pregnant kinswoman, in order to confirm the
faith of Elizabeth. So, too, Mary's intervention at the wedding
feast of Cana sprang from her own initiative. That loving solicitude, that attentive anticipation of others' needs, characterizes the
whole of the Blessed Mother's devotion toward us.

In a sermon about the apparitions of Our Lady of Guadalupe
in 1792, Fr. Antonio Lopez Murto said,

Mary? Our Guadalupana? She loved us before we should love her; she came to seek us out when we were least willing; she lovingly entreated us when we still did not think about it. We did not choose her, no.... Here I can do no less than to put on Mary's lips... the beautiful words that on another occasion her beloved Son proffered (John 15:16): I, of my own volition, lovingly chose you.[51]

This is why St. Bonaventure (+1274) observes, "Not only those, O Lady, offend you who outrage you, but you are also offended by those who neglect to ask your favors."[52] Our Lady is "offended" by this because she is a devoted mother who lives to lavish her maternal love on all of those confided to her by her crucified Son.

A story to illustrate this maternal love: One Friday in July of 1984, twenty-year-old Terry Wallis was out for a drive. The truck he was in veered off the road and plunged into a dried-up riverbed thirty feet below. Terry suffered a horrific head trauma; he was comatose. And he remained in a coma for nineteen years. During those nineteen years Terry's mother Angilee faithfully visited her son, spoke to him, encouraged him, and was in every way present to him as a devoted mother.

On one particular Friday in 2004, Angilee was tending to her son in the rehabilitation center. She asked him, "Who is here?" Terry woke up and said, "Mom."

Terry's miracle gives new meaning to the wonder that filled St. Louis de Montfort's heart: "When will it be that souls breathe Mary as bodies breathe the air?"[53]

chapter two

THE IMMACULATE CONCEPTION
How God Conceives of His Own Goodness

ONE WAY TO UNDERSTAND THE MYSTERY OF THE Immaculate Conception is to think back to the Beijing Summer Olympics, to the day swimmer Michael Phelps won his eighth gold medal. It was August 17, 2008, and the event was the four-hundred-meter medley relay. If Phelps finished first he would break the world record of seven gold medals in a single Olympics, set by Mark Spitz in 1972.

People were bursting with anticipation as they stopped to watch the race on television. Americans *really* wanted Michael Phelps to win. But why?

Most of us have never met Michael Phelps. Yet what Phelps could potentially do that day mattered to us. We *identified* with that awesome athlete. Phelps is from our country: He represented our aspirations and what we hold dear. Even more to the point, he is a member of the human race, and whenever we see any member of the human race excel in a seemingly impossible way, we exult. It *increases* us. We sense that that excellence achieved somehow accrues to us as well.

Phelps's victory was our victory; his triumph was our triumph; his glory, our glory. Somehow we were personally involved—implicated—in his history-making event. His breakthrough established a heretofore unknown degree of human greatness. We could say with pride: "We are the people from whom came the greatest Olympic champion of all time, Michael Phelps!" The "miraculous" gold medal he brandished in some way belongs to us as well.

This dynamic is at the heart of the mystery of the Immaculate Conception. The solemnity celebrates the supernatural fact that when the Blessed Virgin Mary was conceived in the womb of her mother Anne, she was conceived without original sin. At the moment of her biological conception (and ever after), Mary's human existence was endowed with an absolutely immaculate purity. And God worked that miracle of holiness in Mary for us.

Pope Benedict XVI explains how the mystery of the Immaculate Conception is totally other-directed: "Preservation from original sin signifies that Mary reserves no area of being, life, or will for herself as a private possession. Instead, precisely in the total dispossession of self, in giving herself to God, she comes to the true possession of self."[1] The "method" of the Immaculate Conception is our path to "the true possession of self."

For the first time in human history since the Fall, a human being was perpetually preserved from original sin along with all its effects, including concupiscence—"the movement of the sensitive appetite contrary to the operation of the human reason" (*CCC*, 2515)—which unsettles our moral faculties and inclines us to commit sins. And that human perfection is meant for us. As

St. Thomas Aquinas comments, "Sanctifying grace not only repressed all irregular motions in the Blessed Virgin herself, but was also efficacious for others; so that notwithstanding the greatness of her beauty, she was never coveted by others."[2] On the contrary, Mary's sublime beauty attracts us to her, and through her to God.

A Never-Ending Event

The Blessed Virgin Mary remained sinless throughout her entire life. In fact, the event of being immaculately conceived so completely defined the Blessed Virgin Mary that in 1858, when she appeared to Bernadette Soubirous in Lourdes, France, she identified herself by saying, "I am the Immaculate Conception."

This miraculous feat that God accomplished in the human flesh of the Blessed Virgin Mary is a breakthrough event for the entire human race. It establishes an otherwise "inconceivable" excellence and changes the way we think, and act, *and hope!* As Pope John Paul II wrote, "The marvelous work which the Creator achieved in Mary gives men and women the possibility to discover dimensions of their condition which before were not sufficiently perceived."[3]

For this reason the Feast of the Immaculate Conception is a day of elation. St. Anselm notes that all things that are subject to the use of human beings now rejoice in Mary's Immaculate Conception because, through her, "they are in some sense restored to their lost beauty and are endowed with inexpressible new grace."[4]

God deigned to work such an august miracle in St. Anne's little girl in order to form her for her vocation as the Mother of God. St. Bede the Venerable (+735) observes, "No wonder that the Lord, when he was about to redeem the world, began his work with his Mother, so that she, through whom salvation would be put into place for all, would be the first to taste the fruit of salvation from her Child."[5]

Although the doctrine of the Immaculate Conception was solemnly defined as a dogma of the Church in 1854, it is something that we would most likely presuppose to be true (as the Church in fact did for centuries) even if it were not explicitly revealed to us. It just seems logical that if God were to have a mother, it would be only fitting for her to be perfectly pure from the first moment of her existence and ever after.

And yet the Church does explicitly define this Marian dogma and asks her faithful in some places to observe the Solemnity of the Immaculate Conception as a holy day of obligation, which means that important reasons exist for Christians to give earnest attention to the Immaculate Conception of Mary.

Yes, we celebrate this feast in recognition of what God has wrought in the woman destined to be the Mother of God. But to treat the Immaculate Conception merely as the commemoration of an occurrence two thousand years ago threatens to turn this seminal mystery of the faith into an abstraction, blurring its relevance and distancing it from our life. What God does for Mary in this miraculous event he does for us here and now through her.

As Pope John Paul II expressed it, "Mary's unique vocation is inseparable from humanity's vocation."[6] St. Anselm states that, thanks to the Immaculate Conception, "not only does [the universe] feel the unseen presence of God himself,… it sees him openly working and making it holy."[7]

How Come I Am Not Immaculately Conceived?

The Immaculate Conception of Mary is so very wonderful that it might just make us wonder, "Why am *I* not immaculately conceived?" After all, I think I might like to go through life without having lust of the flesh, covetousness for material things, or pride of life that ends in self-assertion (that is, the three kinds of concupiscence). Wouldn't it have been easier for God to make us *all* immaculately conceived?

To get at the answer, we must go back to the beginning. The First Reading for the Feast of the Immaculate Conception is taken from the Genesis account of the Fall. The serpent seduces Adam and Eve. And how does he do so? By tempting them with a *conception* that goes something like this: "God knows that the moment you eat of the fruit your eyes will be opened and you will be like gods. What do you want: your life here in Eden or to be like God?"

What is so utterly diabolical is that the serpent insinuates that the two great desires—to live in obedience to God and to be like God—are mutually exclusive. Sadly, the man and woman give in to the serpent's deceptive conception and thereby forfeit their relationship with God and the very possibility for their eternal happiness. The contamination brought about by the serpent's conception has made them blind to the fact that to possess paradise, to be like God, is *to be in relationship* with God.

God ingeniously restores what was lost through the sin of Adam and Eve by employing the very method through which it became lost. He invites us back to the original friendship with him by way of a conception: Mary, the Immaculate Conception. The conception that leads us back to paradise is a human person! God offers us, again and again unfailingly, what our first parents were so ready to throw away: a relationship with him, that is, our happiness. And to be certain that we will never again misconceive or deprecate that relationship, he offers it to us by means of a mother. The eighth-century Benedictine abbot Ambrose Autpert exclaims, "[I]t is right that we extol [Mary] as blessed in a unique proclamation, since she brought the world a unique relationship [with God]."[8]

Mary, the Immaculate Conception, is herself the living, breathing conception of God's ineffable goodness, truth, beauty, fidelity, compassion, justice, mercy, peace, and love. Mary the Immaculate Conception is the means by which God communicates how he conceives of his own holiness.

Through our relationship with Mary, we can recognize that there is no greater paradise than what the Lord offers us through her. St. John of Damascus (+749), speaking of Mary, says, "The serpent never had any access to this paradise."[9]

Mary, the New Eve, undoes the deception that drastically duped Eve of Eden. The *Catechism* speaks of Adam and Eve becoming afraid of God, "of whom they have *conceived* a distorted image" (*CCC*, 399, emphasis added). In Mary the Immaculate Conception we are given a corrected conception of the image of God: The Mother takes away all our fear in the way that only a mother can.

The desire so deep in us to be like God is fulfilled when we remain obedient to God, united with the Immaculate Conception. The privilege of doing this in a way surpasses the prospect of our being "immaculately conceived," precisely because it leads us to do what Adam and Eve refused to do: to depend on God in total self-donation. In Mary the Immaculate Conception we cannot help but be reminded of what Adam and Eve forgot: God *wants us* to be like him; God himself is the one who planted that desire for divinization in our hearts!

The Immaculate Conception is the Mirror of Justice in whom we see what we are destined to become by saying yes to the conception God proposes in his Mother. Bl. John Henry Newman wrote that justice is "a word denoting all virtues at once, a perfect, virtuous state of soul—righteousness, or moral perfection.... Our Lady is the Mirror of sanctity, holiness, supernatural goodness."[10] St. Anselm expresses it this way: "Blessed Lady, now all creation has been restored to life and rejoices that it is controlled and given splendor [by people] who believe in God.... Through the fullness of the grace that was given you, dead things rejoice in their freedom."[11]

God gives us the mystery of Mary the Immaculate Conception so that we will have the right way to approach all of reality. For everything that we do depends on how we conceive of things.

The Impossible No Longer Inconceivable

The fact of the Immaculate Conception introduces a possibility into the world that otherwise would have remained literally "inconceivable." With the event of the Immaculate Conception —that is, the raising up of a human being untouched by the scourge of sin—God's tender love pierces the pall of human misery and evil. The fact of Mary's fetal existence gives us every reason to rejoice in hope!

The *Catechism* emphatically states that God wishes to make us capable of responding to him, knowing him, and loving him far beyond our own natural capacity. At the same time it acknowledges that we cannot respond to God's divine love by our own powers, but we must hope that God will give us the capacity to love him (see *CCC*, 52, 2090). God does precisely that in the Immaculate Conception! He endows Mary the Immaculate Conception with a capacity to know, love, and respond to him that exceeds ordinary human capacities; and through Our Lady's maternal mediation, he imparts those capacities to us.

As Pope John Paul II once explained it, Mary's unique excellence in the world of grace and her perfection are fruits of the divine benevolence, which seeks to raise everyone to the perfection and holiness that are proper to the adopted children of God.[12]

At the beginning of time, when God created the world, he took a handful of dirt and formed from it Adam to be the image of God. In the re-creation that begins in the Immaculate Conception, God forms from the midst of the muck of human misery one mortal set apart to be the immaculate image of himself, so that once again we might truly image God.

Mary is the way that God conceives of his own blessedness. So much so, St. Anselm says, that by virtue of the blessedness that God gives Mary at the Immaculate Conception, "the Creator himself has been blessed *by creation!*"[13] Through God's loving initiative in the Immaculate Conception, the Lord reverses the downward spiral of human, sin-driven self-destruction. Thanks to the event of the Immaculate Conception, God's goodness has become preeminently present in the world and ultimately accessible to all, offered to us by one whom Christ begs us to call Mother.

What Does the Immaculate Conception Mean for Me?

If the meaning of the Immaculate Conception still seems a little difficult or vague, there is a magnificent story from the Old Testament that can make it clear. The book of Esther tells the tale of a young Jewish girl named Hadassah who was "beautifully formed and lovely to behold" (Esther 2:7, *NAB*). She was living with her people in the land of Persia. The king of Persia, King Ahasuerus, took notice of her and set her apart to be his queen.

In the kingdom lived an evil man, the king's grand vizier, named Haman. He harbored an abominable hatred toward the Jewish people, and he conspired to have them all killed in a mass extermination. By devious means he obtained a royal decree authorizing the pogrom. With its issuance it seemed that the Jews of the kingdom were doomed.

However, Mordecai, the uncle of Hadassah, who was now Queen Esther, learned of the evil plot. He went to his niece and pleaded with her: "You are beautiful and exceptional in so many ways, thanks to God's goodness. And King Ahasuerus has raised you to a prestige and stature that you never could have achieved apart from the extraordinary gifts which are yours due to God's grace alone. You must realize that this privilege was not given to you for yourself alone. You have been blessed with the royal dignity that you now enjoy in preparation for this fateful day, so that you could be the one to save us from the unspeakable evil that threatens us. If you approach King Ahasuerus and beg for his clemency and pardon, he will recognize your surpassing beauty and favor, and he will grant you everything you wish."

That is exactly what Queen Esther did. And by her intervention she saved her people from destruction.

God blesses the Mother of God with the supernal beauty and perfection of the Immaculate Conception so that we will appeal to it when we are threatened or afraid, certain that our queen will intercede on our behalf to the Father. And God, captivated by the beauty that he himself gave to Mary the Immaculate Conception, will hear and heed her.

To think about it in another way, suppose someone wins a hundred million dollars in the lottery today. What will happen to that person tomorrow? He will likely be deluged by phone calls from perfect strangers asking for money. What right do they, perfect strangers, have to ask for a share of his winnings?

But we consider this a completely natural thing, don't we? We say to ourselves, "All that money was a *gift*: He didn't earn it; he did nothing to deserve it. So the best way for him to honor what has been given to him gratuitously is to give some to me!"

That is exactly what God wants us to do as we consider the "fortune" that is the Immaculate Conception.

In 1882 Jane Woolsey Yardley, who had recently lost her husband, decided to build a house for herself and her four children next door to her mother in Newport, Rhode Island. Being financially strapped, she went to a stranger who lived nearby, namely Cornelius Vanderbilt II, and asked him for a loan of $5,000. He granted it, immediately and without interest. In a year Yardley repaid the loan in full, but Vanderbilt sent the young widow a cordial letter releasing her from the debt.[14] It seems that the gratification of being acknowledged, trusted, relied on, and appealed to sufficed for the millionaire.

The same is true in our devotion to Mary the Immaculate Conception. In her unmerited purity and perfection, she is blessed with the treasure of every grace. As St. Louis de Montfort assures us, "[T]his immense treasure is none other than Mary, whom the saints call the treasure of the Lord, by whose plenitude [people] are made rich."[15]

This great mystery is proclaimed and solemnly celebrated by the Church, so that in considering the vast richness who is Mary the Immaculate Conception, we will avail ourselves of her supernatural wealth. St. Anselm exclaims, "Lady, full and overflowing with grace, all creation receives new life from your abundance."[16]

When we listen to the following words of Louis Lavelle and reflect on our lives of faith, we can see that we have been blessed by the purity of Mary the Immaculate Conception: "Purity is a living transparency.... Purity proves its strength and efficacy by passing through all uncleanness in the world without receiving any taint, but rather leaving in its midst its own radiance.... Purity is an act of presence to oneself and to the world."[17]

A New Beginning

The Immaculate Conception testifies to the reality that we cannot think our way into heaven. "Being Christian is not the result of an ethical choice or a lofty idea."[18] The one crucial and indispensable conception for our salvation is Mary the Immaculate Conception. It behooves us to consider the point made by St. Louis de Montfort: "No one is filled with the living thought of God except through Mary."[19]

Pope John Paul II told us that Mary's exalted holiness is to encourage all Christians to open themselves to the sanctifying power of the grace of God.[20] In Mary all are called to put total trust in the divine omnipotence, which transforms hearts, guiding them toward full receptivity of his providential plan of love.

Through the Church's celebration of the Solemnity of the Immaculate Conception, God invites us to leave behind all our inadequate and disappointing preconceptions and to live devoted to his Immaculate Conception, to open ourselves to the sanctifying power of his grace made present in a person we are destined to call mother. Because that kind of obedient surrender to the Immaculate will be the beginning of a newness for us that will never end.

chapter three

THE BIRTH OF MARY
The Birth of the Mother of Our Rebirth

ON WHAT DAY WAS ARISTOTLE'S MOTHER BORN? WHO
knows? And in a way, who really cares?

Aristotle was one of the most esteemed men in history, yet we
have no clue about his mother's birthday. But we *do* know and
celebrate the birthday of the mother of a Jewish carpenter from
an obscure minor nation. The Church has commemorated the
birth of the Blessed Virgin Mary from at least the fifth century,
when a church in honor of Mary's mother, St. Anne, was erected
in Jerusalem.

Maybe the greatness we glean from the heroes of secular history is enough for us. But not when it comes to Christ. There's a
reason why the early Church determined the birthday of the
Mother of God and observed it with fervor and worship: Mary's
birth signals the end of our death. In her beginning is a permanent beginning for us.

We Are Barren No More

In the hymnody of Romanos the Melodist (+556), the Blessed Virgin Mary sings: "Cease your laments; I will make myself your advocate in my Son's presence.... [N]o more sadness, because I have brought joy to the world. For it is to destroy the kingdom of sorrow that I have come into the world: I, full of grace."[1]

Even as Mary lies in her cradle, says St. Peter Julian Eymard (+1868), the demons tremble because they behold the Mother of God advancing against them like a strong army in battle array. Before the newborn Mary the demons feel the humiliation of their leader's defeat and foresee the terrible war that this little girl will wage against them.[2] As Rhineland mystic Bl. John Tauler (+1361) reminds us, in the birth of Mary the

> image of God, which had been lost in Eden, is retrieved, that noble image by which God the Father formed us in his own likeness, and which had been destroyed. She, cooperating with the Father, has given a new birth to all the members of Christ's mystical body, bringing them back to their source, for it is through her that God in his infinite mercy has chosen to lift us all out of the eternal abyss into which, for our part, our sins would have cast us forever.[3]

Rejoicing in this truth, the Byzantine liturgy exclaims:

> In his love for mankind, he who established the heavens in wisdom has fashioned a living heaven. From a barren stem he has brought forth for us his Mother as a branch full of life.... Today the barren gates are opened and the Virgin, the Gate of God, comes forth. Today grace

begins to bear fruit showing forth to the world the
Mother of God, through whom the earth is united to
heaven for the salvation of our souls. Today is the end of
the barrenness of our nature.[4]

The nativity of Mary puts an end to the prolonged sorrow of her
parents, Joachim and Anne, who waited many long and broken-
hearted years for the birth of a child. As St. Gregory Palamas
(+1359) explains:

Why did Mary come from a barren womb? In order to
put an end to her parents' sorrow, transform their dis-
grace, and prefigure that deliverance from the grief and
curse of the Forefathers of the human race, which was to
come about through her. Let us strive to change our
inner thoughts for the better, having as our helper,
through invoking her name, the Virgin who was today
bestowed upon her parents. She transformed their sorrow, annulled the ancestral curse, and brought our first
mother's pangs to an end painlessly bearing Christ as a
Virgin.[5]

Mary's is a birthday to remember because the answer to our sorrow, misery, malice, loneliness, inability, and strife is to be born of
Mary. When Mary is born, says St. Andrew of Crete (+740), "we
are led toward the truth, and we are led away from our condition
of slavery.... How can this be? Darkness yields before the coming
of the light."[6]

St. John Vianney extols Mary: "Your birth, O Blessed Virgin
Mary, fills the whole world with a sweet consolation and a holy
joy, because of you was born our Jesus, our God, who has taken

away from us the curse in which we were plunged by the sin of our first parents, and filled us with all kinds of blessings."[7] And that is why we are eager to know, and to return in the liturgy, to the moment of Mary's birth: so that we can participate totally in the mystery whereby the possibility of our happiness and salvation is born of a woman.

We commemorate then "the birth of the Virgin, with whom is likewise born our salvation."[8] St. Gregory Palamas continues this theme:

> This month our salvation had its origin, as we celebrate today. This sacred feast and holiday that we are keeping is the first to commemorate our recall and re-creation according to grace, for on it all things began to be made new, enduring precepts began to be brought in instead of temporary ones, the spirit instead of the letter, the truth instead of shadows.... Today a new world and a mysterious paradise have been revealed, in which and from which a New Adam came into being, re-making the Old Adam and renewing the universe.[9]

A Living Expression of Christ's Perfections

In reflecting on the nativity of Our Lady, Bishop Bossuet comes to the conclusion that when God created Mary, he was thinking of Jesus. He reasons that, just as when God created the first Adam "he meant to trace out the second," something similar happens in the creation of the Blessed Virgin. "Intending soon to bestow on us His Word Incarnate, on the day of Mary's nativity He gives us an outline—I might almost say a *beginning*—of Jesus Christ, in one who, though a creature, is in some sort a living expression of His own perfections."[10] St. Gregory Palamas recognizes this as well when he exclaims, "Today has sprung up from the earth the true image of human nobility which comes from above."[11]

In the birth of Mary, we see in the flesh the potential of our own perfection. The eighth-century Benedictine monk Paul the Deacon, with great hopefulness, declares, "Mary came forth from us; she is a precious jewel of our race; our honor was perfected in her."[12] St. Bridget of Sweden asserts that God "foreknew from all eternity that, when [Mary was] born, it would be the greatest joy for him."[13] Why? Because God rejoices in both the creation of this perfect image of his divine greatness and in the prospect of the world's salvation through her maternal mediation.

In the birth of Mary we are given the first manifestation of Our Lady's ineffable tenderness. St. Catherine of Siena prays, "When I look at you, O Mary, I see that the hand of the Holy Spirit has written the Trinity in you, forming in you the incarnate Word, the Only-begotten Son of God."[14]

The newness wrought in the world at the birth of this babe goes beyond description. As the poet Rainer Maria Rilke observes,

> Oh what it must have cost the angels
> not suddenly to burst into song, the way one bursts
> into tears…
>
> …For it had never been like this.[15]

The Birth of the Creator's Dwelling Place

Not long ago friends of mine were visiting New York City from Los Angeles. They came originally from Brooklyn, and the first thing they wanted to do when they got back to the East Coast was to drive over to their old neighborhood and look at the house where they grew up. Somehow the act of going back to that hallowed place and remembering reinforced their appreciation and possession of the good things they had received through God's providence in their family.

Such a sacred "place" is given to us at the birth of Mary. St. Andrew of Crete directs us, "Let everything, mundane things and those above, join in festive celebration. Today this created world is raised to the dignity of a holy place for him who made all things. The creature is newly prepared to be a divine dwelling place for the Creator."[16]

On the birthday of Mary, we are "edified" by the singular "edifice" that God erects in our midst. "At last, when the time appointed for the redemption of mankind had come," says St. Louis de Montfort, "Eternal Wisdom built himself a house worthy to be his dwelling-place. He created the most holy Virgin, forming her in the womb of Saint Anne with even greater delight than he had derived from creating the universe."[17]

We need this divine dwelling place who is Mary. For as Bl. Henry Suso (+1366) confesses, "I flee to your shelter, not daring to show myself naked and beggared in the presence of so much light, but with you, my Mother, I take refuge."[18]

Some spiritual writers address this same human need by way of the image of a book to which we have access. St. Gregory Palamas writes: "Today a paradoxical book has been made ready on earth, which in an indescribable way can hold, not the imprint of words, but the living Word himself."[19]

St. Catherine of Siena also employs this imagery:

> Today, O Mary, you have become a book
> in which our rule is written.

In you, today, is written the wisdom
of the eternal Father.
In you, today, is manifested
the strength and freedom of human beings.
Today I ardently make my request,
because it is the day of graces,
and I know that nothing is refused
to you, O Mary.
Today, O Mary, your land has generated
the Savior for us.[20]

In short, it is thanks to this mystery of the birth of Mary that we can begin to do what Christ will command us from the cross: "Behold, your mother."

c h a p t e r   f o u r

THE PRESENTATION OF MARY
Self-Donation as Destiny

HE INSPIRATION FOR THE FEAST OF THE PRESENTATION of Mary (celebrated November 21) comes from certain apocryphal texts (notable ancient writings not included in the official canon of the Bible). According to these accounts, on a given day Joachim and Anne solemnly brought their three-year-old daughter to the temple in order to fulfill a vow and to obtain education for their blessed child.

The gesture is a sublime act of *self-donation*—a ritualized gift of her person, her "I"—that serves to define the very life and vocation of the Blessed Virgin Mary. In one of her revelations, St. Bridget voices Our Lady's thoughts at her presentation: "As the time approached when, by rule, virgins were presented in the temple of the Lord, I went up among them in submission to my parents, thinking that nothing was impossible to God. And as he knew that I desired nothing, wished nothing but himself, he could, if it pleased him, preserve me in my virginity."[1] Through this sacred event Our Lady models the kind of disposition every

Christian is called to have toward God, even from the earliest moments of our life.

In offering Mary to the Lord in the temple, Joachim and Anne are, in effect, presenting the Blessed Virgin to her *destiny*. Fr. Julian Carron, the president of the ecclesial movement Communion and Liberation, gives a good way to understand what we mean by *destiny*:

> Destiny is nothing but the ultimate meaning of reality—what makes it worthwhile that reality exists. When one discovers this meaning, one is attached to this destiny of his because loving destiny means loving oneself truly. Destiny is this urgency we feel inside us—urgency to find what makes being here worthwhile. One cannot perceive reality except in as much as it provokes him to his destiny. Man cannot truly know by himself the nature of his destiny. "Who can go into himself and understand himself?" (St. Ephrem).[2]

Joachim and Anne "take Mary out of herself" by bringing her into the presence of God in the temple. Our commemoration of this mystery of Mary rekindles the urgency in us to discover what is truly worthwhile, what is deeply meaningful, in life. And since we cannot go into ourselves in order to understand ourselves, we go forth with the chosen child Mary, accompanying her into God's dwelling place in the hope that what she encounters there she will share with us.

Mary the Dove

Perhaps the most poignant and profound image conveying the meaning of this mystery is that employed by St. Germanus, the patriarch of Constantinople. St. Germanus compares Mary at her presentation to the dove that Noah released from the ark, to fly off in search of some sign that the flood was over. He writes: "Hail, God's holy throne, divine offering, … and chosen jewel, … the heaven that tells the glory of God, dawn shining with light inaccessible.… [I]n your glorious and splendid Presentation, you bring us the liberating olive branch of the spiritual Flood; Hail, dove: you bring us the glad tidings of the birth of salvation."[3]

The mystery of the Presentation of Mary, then, blesses us with new and certain hope. Mary is chosen by heaven to bear to us the sign that God's mercy has appeared on the earth. In her we learn that we are refugees no longer.

The prospect of our redemption signified in the Presentation of Mary moves the Byzantine liturgy to proclaim:

> Today is the prelude to God's munificence, and the announcement of the salvation of men: in the temple of God the Virgin is seen openly, foretelling to all the coming of Christ. Wherefore let us cry out to her with all our strength: "Joy to you, fulfillment of the Creator's plan!" You are the pride of the martyrs and the cause of the renewal of the entire human race, for through you we have been reconciled with God. Wherefore we honor your entrance into the temple of the Lord, repeating to you the salutation of the angel, for we are saved through your intercession, O most honorable one![4]

The celebration of the Presentation of Mary reminds us how much our life resembles that of the people on Noah's Ark. Alone and adrift, we ache for some sure sign that God has not forgotten us, that there is more to life than empty horizons, that God's mercy is greater than his wrath, that divine providence will show itself in a concrete sign when we need it most. What exultation must have erupted on the ark the moment that little dove flew back to its decks with an olive branch in its beak! Even more, what would the people on the ark have done without this dove?

The Feast of the Presentation of Mary gives us the assurance that God has confided to us someone we can rely on who will convey to us the promise of the Lord's saving love. We send forth this Dove, and she returns bearing in her womb one who carries not an olive leaf but the tree of the cross. This is why Pope John Paul II declares that "the whole of the universe is … touched by the divine favor with which the Father looks upon Mary."[5]

Consecration: Capable of Amazing the World

The Presentation of Mary in the temple is an act of consecration. This feast holds special significance for those persons called to consecrated life in the Church; at the same time it moves all people to reflect on the meaning of consecrated life *for* the Church.

What Pope John Paul II says about consecrated life in his apostolic exhortation *Vita Consecrata* is revealed first and foremost in the life of the Blessed Virgin Mary, especially as Our Lady is presented in the temple:

> The first duty of the consecrated life is *to make visible* the marvels wrought by God in the frail humanity of those who are called. They bear witness to these marvels not so much in words as by the eloquent language of a transfigured life, capable of amazing the world. To people's astonishment they respond by proclaiming the wonders of grace accomplished by the Lord in those whom he loves…. It is the duty of the *consecrated life* to show that

the Incarnate Son of God is… the infinite beauty which
alone can fully satisfy the human heart.[6]

The consecration that Mary both embraces and manifests at her
presentation is all-surpassing. The poet Rainer Maria Rilke gets
to the heart of this mystery when he writes that when Mary

softly climbed, self-confidently,
towards this extravagance…,
everything that humans build
was already diminished by the praise in her heart.[7]

The Three Temples

Mary was presented in the temple because the temple was con-
sidered "the privileged place of encounter with God" (*CCC*, 584).
(In this way the Presentation of Mary is a kind of foreshadowing
of her assumption into heaven.) Yet, as the *Catechism* teaches, the
temple prefigures Christ's own mystery: His body is destined to
become "the definitive temple," "the true temple of God" (see
CCC, 593, 1197).

The Presentation of Mary anticipates this transformation of
the temple from edifice to flesh. Since Jesus is destined to become
the lasting temple, Mary's presentation is a concrete beginning of
her yes to the conception of the Word made flesh. Even though
the temple will change, God's method will not: It is the method
of encounter that we continue to experience through the agency
of Mary. The privileged place of encounter with God—Jesus
Christ our Lord—comes to us from the womb of Mary.

At the same time it is true to say that Mary is presented in the
temple in order to prepare her to *become* a temple. The Church
honors Our Lady in a Mass entitled "The Blessed Virgin Mary,

Temple of the Lord." The Opening Prayer of that Mass asks, "Lord God, with artistry beyond all telling you fashioned a holy temple for your Son in the virginal womb of Blessed Mary; grant that…we may…become like Mary a temple of your glory."[8]

The Byzantine liturgy acclaims this same truth: "The most pure temple of the Savior, his most precious bridal chamber, the Virgin, sacred treasury of God's glory, enters today into the house of the Lord, bringing with her the grace of the divine Spirit. Wherefore the angels of God are singing: 'Behold the heavenly tabernacle!'"[9]

Accordingly, as we celebrate the Presentation of Mary, St. John Eudes exhorts us: "Give thanks to Almighty God who resists the proud and gives grace to the humble, and offer him all the glory that this Maiden accorded to his majesty by her practice of richest humility during her childhood and throughout the rest of her life."[10]

We live Our Lady's grace of the Presentation by making our own the expectation that filled her heart as she approached the sacred precincts. The seventeenth-century Mexican nun and poet Sor Juana Inés de la Cruz expresses it well:

> Girl, hardly had you
> begun to walk,
> when you had
> the desire to fly.…
>
> Up the high steps
> ceaselessly you climb,
> since ascending is for you
> a natural inclination.…

Now enter the temple,
if it's God you're seeking,
and one day he will come
in search of you.[11]

When God finds Mary, may he find us with her, so that we will find our destiny.

chapter five

THE ANNUNCIATION
The Yes That Makes the Impossible Possible

MARY'S PREPARATION FOR THE ANNUNCIATION WAS A kind of presharing in the Passion of Christ. The immaculately conceived virgin bore in her person none of the effects of original sin. Mary never experienced envy. She was never self-serving, never ungrateful or resentful or petty. Mary never told a lie. Yet, in her singular state of purity, Mary came face-to-face every day with others in whom the consequences of original sin were painfully apparent.

The situation must have been a source of consternation for the Blessed Virgin—an occasion of suffering. *Why* was she so unlike other people? And what did that difference mean? How could she endure it?

Mary's sinlessness imbued her life with urgent expectation. Our Lady's "different humanity" impelled her to seek out its reason, to search for Something More. Even in its fallenness all of humanity shares to a degree in that search. The French theologian Bishop Bossuet, writing about the Fall, says,

> Out of that great and terrible wreck, in which human
> reason lost its chief possessions, and especially the Truth
> for which God had formed it, the mind of man has
> retained a vague and uneasy desire to recover some ves-
> tiges of that truth.... [I]t may be asserted of this desire
> for "something new" that throughout the universe no
> feeling has a stronger hold on human nature, or is a more
> common incentive to all forms of activity.[1]

In response to this desire that has the strongest hold on human
nature, God offers himself *in* a human nature. "The angel Gabriel
was sent from God to a city of Galilee named Nazareth, to a virgin;... and the virgin's name was Mary" (Luke 1:26–27). Rainer
Maria Rilke, in a poem about the Annunciation, describes
Gabriel as "an angel with a young man's face."

> [He] bent closely down to her;...his gaze
> and her raised eyes collided....
> And they were both frightened.[2]

What frightens the angel is the purity and humility in Mary
capacious enough to contain what heaven cannot hold. Romanos
the Melodist exclaims, "All of heaven ... is too small to contain
my Lord. And this poor maiden, how will she be able to receive
him?"[3] (In fact, the Byzantine liturgy goes so far as to assert that
"the earth has become heaven" through Mary's *Fiat*.[4])

But what frightens the angel even more is the intensity of
Mary's ardor for God. Bossuet says, "[T]he love and longing of
Mary were in a measure necessary for our salvation."[5] For that
ardent desire of the Blessed Virgin's heart literally drew heaven to
earth. As a result, says St. Ambrose, "she, who felt like a stranger

when in the presence of a man, did not feel strange to be in the presence of an angel."[6] He was the one she had been waiting for all her life. Her immaculate heart was made for this encounter.

God Looks With Favor on the Lowliness of His Servant

More than anything else, what moved God to act was the *humility* he found in the Blessed Virgin. The saints celebrate this. St. Thérèse of Lisieux tells us that "this hidden virtue … [attracted] the Holy Trinity into [the Blessed Virgin Mary's] heart."[7]

St. Catherine of Siena extols the deep humility of Our Lady, praying: "[At the Annunciation] you were overtaken by wonder and surprise at the consideration of your own unworthiness and weakness and of God's unutterable grace.… You felt…wonder at God's boundless goodness and charity toward the lowliness and smallness of your virtue."[8]

Why would God be so attracted by humility? Humility disposes us to the grace of God as does nothing else. Humility creates a space that God can inhabit with his self, healing and perfecting our self. "True humility," wrote the Catholic philosopher Louis Lavelle (+1951),

> is the utter abasement of my whole being to the earth, and it demands of me a supreme uplifting of my soul to God. For no one makes himself naught except to let God fill the void.… Self-contempt deprives us of all our resources, while humility establishes their limits, so that we may use them better.[9]

Monsignor Luigi Giussani (+2005), the founder of the ecclesial movement Communion and Liberation, also stresses this dual dynamic of humility: "Man cannot be humble if on the one hand he refuses his nothingness and if on the other he does not understand and acknowledge the victory of Another, the victorious Presence."[10]

Thus Fr. Raniero Cantalamessa, preacher to the papal household, says, "perfect humility consists in constantly making oneself small, not for the sake of some personal need or benefit, but for the sake of love, to *elevate* others."[11] It was that humility radiating in the soul of Mary that propelled God's love from heaven in the form of an espousal.

Cardinal Joseph Ratzinger makes the point that since "the salvation of the world is exclusively God's doing," it "therefore occurs in the midst of human weakness and powerlessness."[12] This liberating fact leaves us without an alibi for not saying yes with Mary. "It is a surprising but indisputable truth that, amongst the infinite means that God possesses for establishing His glory, the most efficacious of all is necessarily joined to lowliness."[13] Of this we have plenty!

God acknowledges Mary's humility through the gift of his own. Bossuet says that God "can never show His greatness so plainly as when He stoops to humble Himself.... His glory then showed greatest when it corresponded to the depth of His abasement."[14]

God's very *manner of coming* into the world is itself a manifestation of salvation. The Jesuit poet-martyr St. Robert Southwell (+1595) writes,

> Man laboring to ascend procured our fall,
> God yielding to descend cut off our thrall.[15]

All of this is meant to be an encouragement for us who, seeing how undeserving we are of God's goodness, agonize because we have nothing to offer him but our own indigent nothingness. Monsignor Giussani consoles us: "Approaching the Mystery requires only one thing: the awareness of our ineptitude, which is more than nothingness; of our basic incapacity and our continuous betrayal; of our culpable poverty; of our conniving incapacity; of our being nothing."[16] Mary sings in her *Magnificat*, "[The Lord] 'has regarded the low estate of his handmaiden'" (Luke 1:48). This historical fact gives us confidence that God will look upon us similarly in our lowliness.

Hail Mary

In the archangel's two powerful words of greeting, "Hail Mary," everything changes. St. Robert Southwell says,

> Spell Eva back and Ave shall you find,
> The first began, the last reversed our harms.[17]

The salvation of humankind, St. Louis de Montfort tells us, began through the Hail Mary. In a way these words remain the ultimate expression of God's own Marian devotion. According to de Montfort, the Hail Mary is the most perfect compliment that we can offer to Mary, since it is the very compliment that God himself gave in order to win her heart.[18]

Pope John Paul II commented on the words of the Hail Mary: "They could be said to give us a glimpse of God's own wonderment as he contemplates his 'masterpiece'—the Incarnation of the Son."[19] Moreover, de Montfort wrote,

> it was this prayer which caused the Fruit of Life to spring up in this dry and barren world, and…it is this same prayer, devoutly said, which must cause the word of God to germinate in our souls, and to bear the Fruit of

Life, Jesus Christ…. [T]he salvation of each individual soul is linked up with this prayer.[20]

For that angelic utterance, observes Bl. Guerric of Igny, "promises the guilty forgiveness, prisoners redemption, captives liberty, and the buried life. That word strikes fear into hell, gladdens the heavens, and seems to have increased the perfection of the angels by knowledge of mysteries and by new kinds of joy."[21]

A religious sister once told me about a certain orderly in the nursing home she ran. One day the aide was washing an elderly woman patient suffering from Alzheimer's. Even though the orderly couldn't carry on a conversation with his patient, he decided that he would pray for her. So as he washed her arm, he recited the Hail Mary out loud.

All of a sudden the woman fixed his gaze on the man and asked, "Are you praying for me?"

The stunned young man stammered, "Yes,… I am."

The patient replied, "Well,… it's working!"

Mary's Yes

"With a *fiat*," wrote St. Thomas of Villanova (+1555), "God created light, heaven, earth; but with Mary's *fiat*, God became Man."[22] God "came into the world," says St. Leo the Great (+461), "by a new way, for he wished to bring to man's very body a new gift of spotless purity."[23]

Pope John Paul II explained in his encyclical *Redemptoris Mater*: "[I]n Mary's faith … at the Annunciation …, an interior space was reopened within humanity which the eternal Father can fill 'with every spiritual blessing.' It is the space 'of the new and eternal Covenant.'"[24]

Why were the angel's words to be trusted? Because when Gabriel said to Mary, "Do not be afraid" (Luke 1:30), she *stopped being afraid.* The Word of God transfigured her. What the angel announced to her *corresponded* with the deepest longings of her humanity.

The mystical writer Hugh of St. Victor (+1141) observes that the motive leading to natural conception is the mutual love shared between a man and a woman. Since in the Virgin Mary's heart there burned such a great love of the Holy Spirit, it is not surprising, he says, that in her body the same love worked miracles.[25]

Through the mystery of the Annunciation, "God has placed, in the midst of barren, despairing mankind, a new beginning which is not a product of human history but a gift from above," Cardinal Joseph Ratzinger wrote.[26] It is a new beginning *in human flesh*, for if Christ is not real in our lives in a fleshly way, then, Fr. Julian Carron explains, "he becomes more and more something in our imagination. Remembrance is not enough; we need a presence made of flesh, historical, irreducible, that goes on seizing hold of me and drawing me on.... Only Someone who is happening now can draw along my whole life, my whole heart, all my love towards himself."[27] The Annunciation is the inauguration of this new and permanent method by which God ordains to draw all people to himself.

In the Annunciation God breaks through the rebellion and inertia of the world, not with an idea or a doctrine but with his presence in the flesh. Jacob of Serug wrote, "Maiden and Watcher [the angel] met each other and conversed ... until they abolished the conflict between the Lord and Adam."[28]

The marvel of the Annunciation is that Mary agrees to this stupefying method. She respects the freedom of God to save the world in just this way. The insight of the philosopher Gabriel Marcel applies preeminently to Mary: "There is a way of listening that is a way of giving."[29]

Everything distinctive about Mary's "I" convinces her that she has been made for this "You." Mary does not resist; she does not attempt to impose her own method. She lets it happen. Somehow she senses in the experience of her own freedom that "the Word made flesh is the pivot of salvation. An affectively attractive presence in the flesh is the only one capable of overcoming our resistance. A winning attraction is the only hope for us, who are so tempted by the allure of autonomy, of that almost suicidal affirmation of ourselves that leads us to nothingness."[30]

What begins in the body of the Virgin Mary, Model of the Church, continues perpetually in the body that is the Church: To save us, the Father constantly breaks into the world with the presence of his Son through the friendship experienced by the people of God, through Christ's Eucharistic presence, through the witness of the saints, and so on.

Before all else, in the angel's astounding proposal Mary perceives not a problem she needs to solve but the Mystery who *chooses her*. This is why the method of the Annunciation remains *the norm* for all Christian faith. For faith is not something that I think up; it is not the fruit of analysis. Neither does faith equal "keeping rules": It is not the result of my initiatives to get close to God; it is not the outcome of my "ethical excellence." Faith is a response to *something that happens* outside of me. Faith entails acknowledging an exceptional presence that chooses to come to me—a presence that radically changes my life, infusing it with an intensity and fullness I cannot bring about on my own.

The Living Angelus

How do we even know about the Annunciation in the first place?

The only explanation is that the Blessed Mother herself told the first disciples about it. But *why* did the disciples want to know about it? Because they recognized how much their own growth in faith depended upon that providential beginning. They needed personally to participate in that origin, for the Annunciation is an event that never ends, the principle of every person's salvation.

In conceiving Jesus, St. Thomas Aquinas tells us, Mary became in some way "*the source* of that grace which He was to pour forth over all mankind."[31] This is a prominent theme in St. Louis de Montfort's masterpiece *True Devotion to the Blessed Virgin*. The Blessed Trinity "became fruitful through Mary, whom He espoused. ... [W]ith her, in her, and from her, He constantly produces the members of the Mystical Body."[32]

Bossuet says, "God having once elected to give us Jesus Christ through the Blessed Virgin, this order of things can never change .... It is, and always will be, true, that having once received the Author of our salvation through her, we shall necessarily continue to receive help towards that salvation in the same manner."[33]

The mystical masters of the Church tell us that the womb that welcomed God's Son as her own remains forever fertile. Bl. Guerric of Igny wrote, "The womb that once gave birth is not dried up; it continues to bring forth the fruit of her tender compassion. Christ, the blessed fruit of that womb, left his mother still fraught with inexhaustible love, a love that once came forth from her but remains always within her, inundating her with his gifts."[34]

The Benedictine theologian Rupert of Deutz (+1129) comments, "The same Holy Spirit would accomplish the rebirth of many sons of God from the womb of the Church or by means of her womb, in the life-giving bath of his grace."[35] And St. Louis de Montfort adds, "In the highest degree to which a mere creature is capable of receiving it, God the Father communicated to Mary His own fecundity, in order that she might be enabled to bring forth His Son and all the members of His Mystical Body."[36]

This conviction leads the esteemed German Jesuit theologian Hugo Rahner (+1968) to conclude, "There is no moment, no movement of our spiritual life that does not look back in a mystical sense to the womb whence we came. We are always experiencing the rebirth from our mother, since every turn of events is in our life in a real sense the realization, scattered through time and space, of the germ of life derived from our mother."[37]

The Church's faithful and frequent practice of praying the *Angelus* voices this conviction. We pray with a desire not merely to recall what happened to Mary but to be united with her in her surrender to the Mystery, in her gift of self to God. We pray with the hope of identifying personally with the highly favored Blessed Virgin. We beg God's Spirit to act in our life as he did in that of Our Lady.

St. Louis de Montfort promises us that "when the Holy Spirit finds His Spouse [Mary] in a soul, He flies to that soul to communicate Himself to it, to fill it with His Presence, in proportion as He discovers therein the presence and the fullness of His Spouse.... [T]he more the Holy [Spirit] finds Mary...in a soul, the more powerfully He works to produce Jesus Christ in that soul, and that soul in Jesus Christ."[38]

St. Ildephonsus of Toledo captures the attitude with which we worthily pray the *Angelus*:

> Holy Virgin, I beg you:
> enable me to receive Jesus from the Spirit,
> according to the same process
> by which you bore Jesus....
> May I love Jesus
> in the Spirit
> in Whom you adored Him as your Lord
> and looked after Him as your Son.[39]

The Annunciation teaches us that, no matter how great may be our weakness, God asks only that we surrender to our heart's desire for the Infinite and yield to the Infinite's presence when he comes to meet us in the flesh. At the Annunciation God asked Mary to be his mother. And at the crucifixion he asked Mary to be a mother again, now in a new way: "Behold, your son" (John 19:26).

St. Ambrose says, "So great was [Mary's] grace, that not only it preserved her own virginity, but conferred that admirable gift of purity on those who beheld her."[40] Waiting with Mary's own Annunciation expectation, we behold our Mother. And with all the love and the longing with which Mary once waited for an angel, Mary turns her maternal attention to us.

chapter six

THE VISITATION
How the Closeness of Jesus Comes Close to Us

ONCE THE WORD BECOMES FLESH AT THE ANNUNCIATION, Mary begins to move. The Church calls her movement the "Visitation." What makes a visitation different from a simple visit is that it intends to accomplish something. A visitation is an encounter that *carries within it a meaning that is significant or even exceptional.*

What is the meaning of the Visitation? For we can be sure that it is meant for us!

An Approach and a Presence

At the Annunciation, says St. Bonaventure, "the Creator of all things rests in the tabernacle of the virginal womb."[1] The Visitation is the first Corpus Christi procession. The Blessed Virgin's initial impulse, once God takes up residence in her body, is to bear that presence to others. Pope Benedict tells us, "What we need is the presence in our lives of what is real and permanent so that we can approach it."[2] We can approach the real and permanent presence of Jesus Christ because Our Lady of the Visitation first approaches us.

How critical presence is to our well-being! The philosopher Gabriel Marcel (+1973) wrote that "when somebody's presence does really make itself felt, it can refresh my inner being, it reveals me to myself, it makes me more fully myself than I should be if I were not exposed to its impact."[3] We experience what makes us human in our capacity for being open to others. As the modern theologian Ralph Harper (+1996) contends, "The paradox of the mystery of presence is that while it cannot be comprehended, in that sense cannot be handled, it can be the source of life and in that sense touched."[4]

To be human is to *be* expectation—that is, to be human is to be a state of waiting for One who will come to reveal life's meaning to us. And a person responds, Lavelle tells us, "with total confidence and joy to one who would draw him towards an invisible presence, a presence from which he draws strength; for when another makes him aware of it, that presence ceases to be an illusion, a fiction, or a mere hope, and becomes the very presence of the living God."[5] In the Visitation the Mother of God draws us toward that invisible presence who is our strength.

Setting Before Us the Mysteries of God's Son

"Mary set out, proceeding in haste into the hill country to a town of Judah" (Luke 1:39, *NAB*). To "set out"—literally, to "arise"—is an important action in Luke. This verb is used in the Gospel to indicate Jesus' resurrection as well as any physical actions that imply spiritual effort. Thus, Jesus arose—set out—from the synagogue to heal Peter's mother-in-law (see Luke 4:38). The repentant prodigal son arises—sets out—to return to his father's house

(Luke 15:18, 20). Peter rises—sets out—for the tomb of Jesus, which he discovers empty (Luke 24:12). And the two disciples on the road to Emmaus rise—set out—to go back to Jerusalem after they encounter the risen Christ in the breaking of the bread (Luke 24:33).

Clearly then the "setting out" of the Blessed Virgin Mary at the Visitation anticipates all the healing, all the reconciliation, all the resurrected newness, all the resolute hope that flow from the coming of the kingdom of God. Similarly, those who proceed "in haste" in the Gospel of Luke are the shepherds who hasten to find the Holy Family (Luke 2:16) and Zacchaeus, who hurries down out of his tree when Christ announces his plan to stay with him (Luke 19:5–6). Mary's traveling in haste prefigures the transformation promised those who make Christ's presence their priority. Poet Rainer Maria Rilke says, "Walking on, she realized: no one could go beyond the power that she now experienced."[6]

This impetus that Mary exhibits in the Visitation never ends. Bishop Bossuet explains:

> The visit that so honored and overwhelmed Elizabeth had not been sought by her: part of the very honor consisted in the fact that Mary had paid it of her own accord.... Our God treats us, His poor creatures, in the same way. Whether the sinner who needs converting, or the just who is called to a higher life and the way of perfection, be concerned, He alike comes without waiting for us to ask Him. We are often not thinking of Him specifically at all—we may have even actually forgotten Him; but He *seeks us out*—goes before us—or, as sacred language has it, "prevents" us: we feel and know His

grace, suddenly present with us, as the Baptist knew it in his mother's womb, when we have done absolutely nothing to call it down.[7]

The many approved Marian apparitions that have taken place in the world throughout the Church's history find their scriptural foundation in the mystery of the Visitation. As Pope John Paul II reminded us, "Mary constantly sets before the faithful the 'mysteries' of her Son, with the desire that the contemplation of those mysteries will release all their saving power."[8]

Our Lady does this literally in the Visitation. She makes her journey in order to generate in all people the union of love that she experiences with the Son in her womb. She brings to us the nearness of God made flesh. Her constant maternal initiatives in our life remind us of the utter closeness Christ desires to live with us. Every mystery of the Son's life manifests Jesus' desire for ultimate communion with his followers, for which he prayed so ardently the night before he died (see John 17:20–23).

Leaping and Dancing

According to published news reports, the night that Abraham Lincoln was elected president of the United States, "men danced who had never danced before."[9] Some events in life are so electrifying that they move us to act in ways we never imagined. Such is the case with the Visitation.

The spiritual masters of the Church compare the leaping of John the Baptist in his mother's womb with the "leaping and dancing" of David before the ark of the covenant (see 2 Samuel 6:14–16). For Mary in the Visitation comes bearing the Answer to all of life's big questions. This leads the spiritual writer Caryll Houselander (+1954) to say: "It seems that this is Christ's favorite way of being recognized: that he prefers to be known, not by his own human features, but by the quickening of his own life in the heart, which is the response to his coming."[10]

Bishop Bossuet comments that John the Baptist's transports of joy within his mother's womb were caused by *longing*: "He desires liberty for one thing only—that he may fly to his Savior."[11] With this arrival of the One for whom all the world has been eagerly waiting, St. Athanasius tells us, "the Holy Spirit …incites him who is in Elizabeth's womb, as one urges on his friend, 'Hurry, get up!'"[12]

Commenting on the sublime gratuitousness of Mary's charity in the Visitation, St. Ambrose notes that "the grace given to Mary was so great that it…conferred the gift of innocence on those she visited."[13] Peter Chrysologus expresses it this way:

> God's gracious favor toward us was so great that it is impossible for a creature to decide which deserves the most amazement: that God has lowered himself to our level of servitude, or that God has carried us off to the dignity of his divinity. This is why, O man, divinity comes into contact with you, why it is aflame now with such great love for you, why through the words you speak God adopts you as a son while you are still in the womb.[14]

We Are Like Elizabeth

St. Ambrose compares Elizabeth's experience of the Visitation to that of her son John:

> Elizabeth was the first to hear the voice; but John was the first to experience grace. She heard according to the

order of nature; he leaped because of the mystery. She recognized the arrival of Mary; he, the arrival of the Lord. The woman recognized the woman's arrival; the child, that of the child. The women speak of grace; the babies make it effective from within to the advantage of the mothers who, by a double miracle, prophesy under the inspiration of their babies. The infant leaped. The mother was filled with the Holy Spirit. The mother was not filled before the son; but after the son was filled with the Holy Spirit, he filled his mother too. John leaped and the spirit of Mary rejoiced. Elizabeth was filled with the Spirit after she had conceived, and Mary before. But you too, who have heard and have believed are blessed. Every soul who has believed both conceives and generates the Word of God and recognizes his works.[15]

As we ponder the mystery of the Visitation, many of us identify most with Elizabeth. She suffered much in her life because of her barrenness: suffered from powerlessness, from confusion, from alienation, from sorrow, perhaps from resentment and doubt. But something happened in her. Through a miracle of mercy, an impossible life was conceived in her. And thanks to the power of that life, Elizabeth refused to define herself by barrenness any longer. Instead, filled with heaven's promise, she searched the horizon, she looked beyond the hills for a face that would come to help her verify the miracle of grace welling up within her.

The Blessed Mother placed in front of Elizabeth the Mystery made flesh who puts to flight all nihilism, all fatalism, and the dread we feel over our limitations and inadequacies. The divine Presence whom Mary carried caused her cousin *to expect even more* than the truly awesome miracles she had already experienced in her life. She was moved to join her yes to the Virgin's, when Mary sang in her *Magnificat* that God lifts up the lowly, fills the hungry with good things, and comes to the help of those who are his servants.

Our Lady of the Visitation continues to remind us of God's promise of mercy. All that is required is that we do what Elizabeth did as Mary unfailingly makes her way to us: that we welcome the Blessed Virgin Mary into our home.

St. Louis de Montfort encourages us in this: "You can cast yourself down, in spirit, with a profound sense of your own nothingness in the presence of Jesus living in Mary."[16] Bossuet adds, "When God deigns to look upon us, we can but learn from Elizabeth how to reverence His supreme greatness by fully recognizing our own nothingness, and to acknowledge His benefits by confessing our unworthiness."[17]

Nothing could be holier than such humble dependence on the agency of the Mother of God. This is why St. Francis de Sales counsels us:

> Observe that Saint Elizabeth receives the Holy Spirit through the intervention of the Blessed Virgin, in order to teach us that we must make use of her as our Mediatrix with her Divine Son, if we wish to obtain the Holy Spirit. True, we could go directly to God and ask Him for His grace without the help of the Blessed Virgin and the saints, but God has not so willed it.[18]

The keynote of the mystery of the Visitation is *hiddenness*. Bossuet writes:

The events of [the Visitation] bring before the faithful in a peculiar manner the fact that our God is *a hidden God*, and that His power works in the soul in a secret and impenetrable manner.... Our Lord here hides His power intentionally, to show us how He is the invisible force that moves all things without moving Himself, and directs all things without showing His Hand.... His influence is fully apparent in the actions of the rest, whose movements are really all inspired by Him alone.

One of the greatest mysteries of Christianity is the holy union that the Son of God forms with us, and His secret way of visiting us.[19]

The *effects* of the "invisible force," however, cannot be hidden. We see them in the words that the fifth-century spiritual master Jacob of Serug puts on Elizabeth's lips:

An ocean is enclosed in you, Mary, for the earth is too small to contain it; by it, sin is drowned which had overwhelmed all mankind.... That one whom you carry, behold he grows in you, yet he enriches you. Gabriel did not reveal the mystery, but the babe who is in me is the sharer of that secret which you have borne. He shows to me that his Lord dwells in you, O blessed one; from him I have learned who he is and whose Son, and how he is. Since I saw you, he has not ceased urging me to bless you, to do reverence, to rejoice with his Lord who has come to him. As soon as the greeting came to my ears from your lips, the babe whom I carry leaped in me with great joy. He shook in me and I trembled, and he danced in me and I marveled at you; behold, the King, his Lord, quickens me to worship.[20]

Perhaps it was Christ's memory of the story of the Visitation, told to him when he was a child, that moved him to stop, look into a tree, and call out to the man hiding up there, "Hurry down, Zacchaeus! I mean to stay with you today." For nothing changes us as does the One who comes to stay with us. And he comes to us through Mary.

chapter seven

MARY THE MOTHER OF GOD
The Mother We Need for Life

ADAM WAS THE ONLY MAN IN HISTORY WHO DID NOT have a mother. God saw what a mess it got him into and made sure that *that* never happened again. As a result of Adam's sin, God would save humankind, and salvation would have a mother.

Paul of Tarsus, the onetime archenemy of Christianity turned convert, expresses his supreme fascination with the fact that the Son of God has a mother: "But when the time had fully come, God sent forth his Son, born of woman,... so that we might receive adoption as sons" (Galatians 4:4–5).

It did not have to be this way; Jesus could have just "appeared" on earth, as did the Old Testament priest-king Melchizedek, who was "without father or mother or genealogy, and has neither beginning of days nor end of life" (Hebrews 7:3). But God the Father intentionally and purposefully gave his Son a mother in the Incarnation. Why?

Mary's Motherhood and the Father's Love

Pope John Paul II says that Mary "has been granted an utterly special likeness between her motherhood and the divine fatherhood.... The primary effect of the Father's love...is the divine motherhood."[1] For in the order of grace, as in the natural order, says St. Louis de Montfort, a child must have a father and a mother: "All...true...children of God have God for their Father and Mary for their Mother."[2]

Thomas Aquinas points out that "the Blessed Virgin, by becoming the Mother of God, received a kind of infinite dignity because God is infinite; this dignity therefore is such a reality that a better is not possible, just as nothing can be better than God."[3] The Father's gift of the motherhood of Mary is in a way "proto-eucharistic"—that is, the maternity of Mary becomes a unique means by which we are able to receive the *self* of Jesus Christ more perfectly.

God gives a mother to his Son *for us*. Whatever to our minds makes God seem abstract, distant, aloof, elusive, unapproachable, or intimidating is overcome in a mother. "God was absolutely incomprehensible and inaccessible, invisible and inconceivable," wrote St. Bernard of Clairvaux. "But now he wanted to be grasped, seen, and conceived. 'But how?' you ask. Lying in the manger, reclining in his mother's virginal lap."[4] As Pope John Paul II noted, "God chose a virgin mother for his Son to offer his fatherly love more generously to humanity."[5] St. Germanus of Constantinople rightly asks the Blessed Mother, "Who, after your Son, is as interested in humanity as you are?"[6]

Although the theology of the divine maternity of Mary is rich and complex, its meaning becomes clear as we consider our own *experience*. For example: When things go wrong, where would we turn without our mothers? It is a documented fact that dying soldiers on battlefields automatically cry out for their mothers. Most likely it is not that they expect their mothers to materialize. (The Latin word for *mother*—*mater*—is the root of the word *matter*.) But something profound in their experience of having a mother comes to help them in their hour of death.

In 1864, at the height of the Civil War, the composer George F. Root wrote a song entitled "Just Before the Battle, Mother." It became a favorite of the soldiers of both the North *and* the South.

> Just before the battle, Mother,
> I am thinking most of you,
> while upon the field we're watching,
> with the enemy in view.
> Comrades brave around me lying,
> filled with thoughts of home and God,
> for well they know that on the morrow,
> some will sleep beneath the sod.
>
> Farewell, Mother, you may never,
> press me to your heart again;
> but, oh, you'll not forget me, Mother,
> if I'm numbered with the slain.[7]

The song recognizes something almost supernatural about a mother's love that can be relied on to give troops the certainty they need to face even the most harrowing horrors of war. God the Father provides that very consolation to the humanity of his dying Son. The torture of Christ's death was ameliorated to the extent that Jesus could cry out to his mother. Mary's presence at the cross gave Jesus even greater courage to embrace his crucifixion. And our Lord was consoled by the fact that he could give us his mother to be our mother. For good reason we conclude the Hail Mary with the petition, "Pray for us…at the hour of our death."

If Christ had not given us his mother to be our mother, wouldn't we have pined for such a relationship? In recounting her life, St. Teresa of Avila wrote:

> I remember that when my mother died I was twelve years old or a little less. When I began to understand what I had lost, I went, afflicted, before an image of our Lady and besought her with many tears to be my mother. It seems to me that although I did this in simplicity it helped me. For I have found favor with this sovereign Virgin in everything I have asked of her, and in the end she has drawn me to herself.[8]

Mother of Total Life

This natural impulse to look beyond ourselves when confronted by our limitations is at the root of the mystery of the motherhood of Mary. From an infant's first moments on earth, the baby searches the face of his or her mother. The psychiatrist Alice Miller describes this dynamic in her compelling book *The Drama of the Gifted Child: The Search for the True Self*:

> Every child has a legitimate need to be noticed, understood, taken seriously, and respected by his mother. In the first weeks and months of life he needs to have the mother at his disposal, must be able to avail himself of her and to be mirrored by her…. [T]he mother gazes at the baby in her arms, and the baby gazes at his mother's face and finds himself therein…provided that the

mother is really looking at the unique, small, helpless being and not projecting her own expectations, fears, and plans for the child. In that case, the child would not find himself in his mother's face, but rather the mother's own predicaments. This child would remain without a mirror, and for the rest of his life would be seeking this mirror in vain.[9]

Despite the excellence of our mothers, we persist nonetheless in looking for that *ultimate* maternal mirror in which we can discover ourselves to our deepest depths. Mary's is the face we seek.

For we cannot understand ourselves and *be* ourselves if left to ourselves. To be ourselves we need someone else. This conviction is a recurrent theme in the writings of Pope Benedict XVI:

Of ourselves, we cannot come to terms with ourselves. Our *I* becomes acceptable to us only if it has first become acceptable to another *I*. We can love ourselves only if we have first been loved by someone else. The life a mother gives to her child is not just physical life; she gives total life when she takes the child's tears and turns them into smiles. It is only when life has been accepted and is perceived as accepted that it becomes also acceptable. Man is that strange creature that needs not just physical birth but also appreciation if he is to subsist.... If an individual is to accept himself, someone must say to him: "It is good that you exist"—must say it, not with words, but with that act of the entire being that we call love. For it is the way of love to will the other's existence and, at the same time, to bring that existence forth again. The key to the *I* lies with the *you*.[10]

Mary, Mother and Model of the Church, is our way of *belonging*. In the gift of Mary's motherhood, which Christ makes personally to every individual on Calvary, the Christian welcomes the Mother of God "into his own home," and as Pope John Paul II comments, "brings her into everything that makes up the Christian's inner life, that is to say into his human and Christian 'I.'"[11] Cardinal Joseph Ratzinger elaborates on this:

> We receive our life not only at the moment of birth but every day from without—from others who are not ourselves but who nonetheless somehow pertain to us. Human beings have their selves not only in themselves but also outside of themselves: they live in those whom they love and in those who love them and to whom they are "present." Human beings are relational, and they possess their lives—themselves—only by way of relationship. I alone am not myself, but only in and with you am I myself.[12]

St. Thérèse of Lisieux understood uncannily how this truth applies to our relationship with the Mother of God:

> With regard to the Blessed Virgin, I must confide to you one of my simple ways with her: I surprise myself at times by saying to her: "But good Blessed Virgin, I find I am more blessed than you, for I have you for Mother, and you do not have a Blessed Virgin to love.... It is true you are the Mother of Jesus, but this Jesus you have given entirely to us...and he, on the cross, he gave you to us as Mother. Thus we are richer than you since we possess Jesus and since you are ours also."[13]

Always Our Mother

A mother is much more than a birth-giver. "Motherhood," writes Pope John Paul II, "is a relationship of person to person: a mother is not only mother of the body or of the physical creature born of her womb, but of the person she begets.... Mary is the *Theotokos* [God bearer] not only because she conceived and gave birth to the Son of God, but also because she accompanied him in his human growth."[14] Hans Urs von Balthasar says that "it was through his Mother that the Lord learned what human love means."[15]

A poignant—and very sad—example of this understanding of motherhood appeared in a magazine article some years ago. A young man named Nick Beavers was born to a wealthy New York socialite family. From his high school days, Nick led a prodigal life, abusing alcohol and drugs to the point of addiction. He made several attempts at rehabilitation.

At the age of thirty, in 1994, Nick learned that his mother was terminally ill with cancer. From a rehab center in Minneapolis, he wrote her a letter (which, tragically, he never sent):

> Dear Ma,
> It seems like years since I last wrote you.... You've got-ten very sick, I've relapsed and now I'm deep in recovery again—as I pray you are. And I do pray....
> Because of my many pathetic charades, you couldn't have known how much I needed you. But I'm telling you now, without you I would not be alive. How hard it was for me to return your constant undying love....
> I will withstand my disease and whatever else befalls me, because you are my mother. But most of all, I love

you and will one day love myself, because you are my mother.

Love, Nick[16]

No matter how lost we are, no matter how conflicted, no matter how troubled, we are hopeful in the knowledge that we have been given a mother who loves us with a constant, undying love. We can withstand whatever befalls us because Mary is our mother. This makes St. Germanus of Constantinople exclaim, "Everything about you, O Mother of God, …exceeds our reason and our faculties."[17]

St. Bernardine of Siena (+1444) believes that in the same moment when Mary consented to become the Mother of God, she also consented to become the mother of all the children of God, bearing them already from that time beneath her heart.[18] The confident hope that Nick Beavers expressed in his heart-breaking letter appeared in a much earlier terra cotta inscription:

> O Immaculate Virgin,
> Mother of God,
> full of grace.…
>
> In your Motherhood
> you have nurtured all human beings.[19]

Why do mothers possess the ability to raise us up from the most abysmal darkness? Because there is nothing abstract about a mother's love; in the love of a mother we are given a face that emboldens us to face whatever imperils us. This remains pre-eminently so in the case of the Mother of God. Von Balthasar says that "in every respect, Mary has the role of concretizer.… Without her the Lord becomes an abstract principle of redemption."[20]

This explains a discovery that Pope John Paul II made at a turning point in his life: "I was already convinced that *Mary leads us to Christ*, but at the time I began to realize also that *Christ leads us to his Mother*."[21] At the most excruciating moment of his passion, Christ commands us to behold his mother as our mother. He leads us to her to reveal how crucial recourse to her is for our life; in our relationship with the Mother of God, the Christ we seek becomes concrete.

St. Bridget of Sweden describes a revelation in which the Blessed Mother appeared and explained to her that, while she was nursing the baby Jesus, the newborn's beauty was so evident and great that all those who looked upon him were relieved of any sorrow they had in their hearts. It prompted the locals to say to one another, "Let us go to see Mary's Son, that we may be consoled."[22] Christ leads us to his mother, that we may experience that consolation of his concrete presence.

Mother Because Virgin

The great mystical writers of the Church concur that "Mary is Mother because she is Virgin; the total gift of her person is the material out of which the Holy Spirit creates the new man who is the Son of God and who will redeem mankind vicariously through his total divine-human gift of self."[23] Our Lady's love makes all the difference in our lives because, as the Virgin Mother of God, Mary loves us in a *virginal* way.

What does it mean to love "virginally"?

Virginal loving is loving according to the truth of things, without imposing our own preconceptions or prejudgments on them. Virginity entails looking at things *without reducing them.* A virgin wants to love without spoiling, to love in a way that preserves what is pristine. Think of the gingerly way you treat a new car once you get it home, so that its "newness" will last; that is virginal!

A virginal heart is struck by the awesomeness of life and the fact that we have a destiny—that we are "made for something," for happiness! Virginity means loving others precisely according to their destiny. To love in a virginal way, one must love without possessing, without manipulating, preserving the proper detachment needed for the experience of love to be full and pure. True virginity is the awareness of the presence of Jesus Christ in all relationships. Virginal loving is a manifestation of the tenderness of the divine mystery.

In order to comprehend virginal love, just think about how *you* want to be loved. Who has ever looked at you this way, loved you this way? That is how the Virgin Mary as Mother loves you.

Maternal Mediation

Pope John Paul II states: "Mary is not only the model and figure of the Church; she is much more…. The Church *draws* abundantly…from the maternal mediation which is characteristic of Mary."[24]

What is this maternal mediation? "Mary's…unique excellence in the world," writes John Paul elsewhere, is a way that the "divine benevolence…seeks to raise everyone to the moral perfection and holiness…proper to the adopted children of God."[25] Since we are not immaculately conceived and we exhibit the effects of original sin (not to mention our *actual* sins!), we are unworthy, as St. Louis de Montfort points out, to receive the Son of God immediately from the hands of the Father: "[T]he Father…gave that Son to Mary, in order that the world should receive him through her."[26]

This divine method has never ceased. The purity by which we are raised to the perfection proper to the children of God is given to us through the maternal mediation of the Mother of God. Mary mediates by elevating us impure and fallen creatures to the dignity of her Immaculate being through her loving us. Mary's maternal mediation makes us worthy of the kind of union with Jesus that she experienced at the Annunciation. Our Lady imparts her unique excellence, her moral perfection, her holiness to us as her children.

St. Thérèse of Lisieux expresses this beautifully: "I do not tremble when I see my weakness, for the treasures of a mother belong also to her child, and I am your child, O dear Mother Mary."[27]

The great master of Marian devotion St. Louis de Montfort calls on an Old Testament narrative to illustrate Mary's mediation. Chapter 27 of Genesis tells the story of the aged Isaac. The patriarch wishes to bless his children before dying. He intends to reserve his special blessing for his firstborn son, Esau. The next in line is Esau's twin, Jacob.

Isaac sends Esau out to hunt; Esau's mission is to return with game and prepare his father a savory meal. Isaac plans to eat the meal, bless his firstborn, and then die.

This gives Rebecca, Isaac's wife, an idea. While Esau is out hunting, she fixes a delicious dish from the family's flock. She then disguises Jacob in his brother's garment, covering him with furs to simulate the rough skin of his brother, and leads him to the elderly Isaac, whose eyesight is failing. Believing this boy to be his older son, Isaac imparts the blessing for his firstborn to Jacob instead of Esau.

Commenting on this episode, which he reads as a parable, St. Louis de Montfort says of Mary:

This good Mother takes us in hand and makes us worthy to appear before the Heavenly Father. She clothes us with the proper garments…of the Elder Brother—that is to say, of Jesus Christ her Son—which she keeps in her…power…. [S]he adorns [her servants] with the merits and the value of their own actions…. She gives …a new beauty to their garments and their ornaments, by clothing her servants with those garments of her own merits and virtues….

…Mary obtains for her servants the blessing of the Heavenly Father…. [T]hey draw near with confidence to the couch of their Heavenly Father. This good Father …tastes with joy what Mary, their Mother, has prepared for Him. Recognizing in them the merits and the good odor of His Son and of the Holy Mother of His Son, He gives them…His blessing.[28]

Just as Jacob went along with this providential plan of his mother, so do Christians give themselves to the Mother of God "in order that she may dress them to the taste of the Heavenly Father, and to His greater glory—of which she knows more than does any other mere creature."[29]

Through her graced maternal mediation, the Mother of God removes all our alibis for not going to God. If we feel unworthy, if we are wracked with guilt, if we are overwhelmed by our nothingness, if the circumstances of our life seem to conspire against our happiness, Mary the Mother of God presents us to God the Father as if we were her only Son.

This maternal mediation asks something of our humility and our freedom. Through our Marian devotion, says St. Louis de Montfort, "we offer and consecrate all that we are and all that we possess to the Blessed Virgin, in order that, through her mediation, Our Lord may receive the glory and the gratitude which we owe Him."[30]

By means of this gesture, we acknowledge a truth that resounds unequivocally in Marian theology throughout the ages: "After God, Mary is the origin, Mother, and generous giver of all the gifts that are granted to us; for to her has the kingdom of mercy been handed over, and through her hands God gives and has decided to give whatever grace he bestows on us."[31] This prompts St. Germanus of Constantinople to sing: "No one is saved, O Blessed Virgin, if it is not through you. No one is freed from evil but through you, O Immaculate Mother. No one receives divine gifts, O Most Pure, but through your mediation. No one is granted the gift of mercy and of grace, but through you, O Sovereign Lady."[32]

But what if, for whatever reason, I neglect to take recourse to the maternal mediation of Mary? Dante answers this quandary famously in *The Divine Comedy*:

> O Virgin Mother, …
> …your loving kindness not only comes to the aid of those who ask for it but very often spontaneously precedes the request for it.[33]

Conclusion

To be totally human we need a mother to love us who is the Mother of God. For whenever Mary loves us, she gives us Jesus. "God the Son desires to be formed and, as it were, to be incarnated daily, through His Mother, in His members," de Montfort tells us.[34] Bl. Guerric Igny sums up for us in his own inimitable eloquence all that we have been trying to say about the graces of the mystery of Mary, the Mother of God:

> Now Mary embraces that only Son of hers in all his members. She is not ashamed to be called the Mother of all those in whom she recognizes that Christ her Son has been or is on the point of being formed. Like the Church of which she is the model, Mary is the Mother of all who are born again to new life. She is the Mother of him who is the Life by which all things live; when she bore him, she gave new birth in a sense to all who were to live by his life.[35]

chapter eight

OUR LADY OF SORROWS
Our Companion in Compassion

W HAT TORTURE CAN COMPARE TO THAT OF A MOTHER witnessing the murder of her own child? The Blessed Virgin Mary subjected herself to just that at the crucifixion of Jesus.

The Mother of God's presence at her Son's slaying recalls one of the most horrifying stories in the Bible. The seventh chapter of the Second book of Maccabees relates the gruesome account of the martyrdom of seven Jewish brothers and their mother by King Antiochus. As Our Lady of Sorrows stood before the crucified Christ, her pierced heart may well have been filled with the sentiments of the mother of the Jewish martyrs, who said to her sons:

> I do not know how you came into existence in my
> womb; it was not I who gave you the breath of life, nor
> was it I who set in order the elements of which each of
> you is composed. Therefore, since it is the Creator of the

universe who shapes each man's beginning, as he brings about the origin of everything, he, in his mercy, will give you back both breath and life, because you now disregard yourselves for the sake of his law. (2 Maccabees 7:22–23, *NAB*)

Most poignant are the words the mother addresses to her seventh son:

I beg you, child, to look at the heavens and the earth and see all that is in them; then you will know that God did not make them out of existing things; and in the same way the human race came into existence. Do not be afraid of this executioner, but be worthy of your brothers and accept death, so that in the time of mercy I may receive you again with them. (2 Maccabees 7:28–29)

What enabled Mary to stay close to Jesus on Calvary?

Despite the enormity of evil and anguish, there was something even greater present that kept the Blessed Mother by Jesus' side. It was the promise of a love that exceeds the horrific weight of human sinfulness. Our Lady of Sorrows saw beyond the abomination, and it was that sight—that certainty—that made her steadfast at the cross. For the Blessed Virgin was destined to be the mother of the indestructible love that would be born from the destruction of her Son. The hope of that unseen chance held Mary fast in the face of an atrocity that goes beyond what anyone can fathom.

Pope John Paul II asserted, "Mary's hope at the foot of the cross contained a light stronger than the darkness that reigns in many hearts. In the presence of the redeeming sacrifice, the hope of the Church and of humanity was born in Mary."[1]

Our Lady of Redemptive Suffering

Bishop Bossuet, verifying the age-old wisdom of the Church, wrote of Christ's passion:

> Mary is appointed to share in this great sacrifice, and to offer up her own Son; and this is why she...gathers up her full strength and stands composed and upright beneath the Cross. This is why, despite all her sufferings, she gives Him with her whole heart to the Eternal Father.... It was the eternal Father's will that Mary should be not only offered in sacrifice with that innocent victim, and nailed to the Cross by the very same nails that pierced His flesh, but that she should share in the accomplishment of the whole mystery wrought by His death.[2]

St. Alphonsus Liguori adds that Mary gave Jesus to us "a thousand and a thousand times, during the three hours preceding His death, and which she spent at the foot of the Cross; for during the whole of that time she unceasingly offered, with the extreme of sorrow and the extreme of love, the life of her Son in our behalf."[3]

The offering Mary made on Calvary was not a first for the Mother of God; Bossuet says that throughout her life Mary had been offering her Son unceasingly from the moment of his presentation in the temple. And there was a certain unique and terrible quality to that suffering: She "had always had to endure the double torment of knowing that He *must* suffer, and of being in uncertainty as to how: so that she herself, as Jesus grew up under her eyes, suffered His passion over and over again, in anticipation that was all the more terrible from being vague."[4]

So committed was the Mother of God to fulfilling the will of the Father regarding Christ that she not only permitted the death of her Son but fully consented to it. As St. Bonaventure explains:

> When she saw the love [of] the Eternal Father towards [people] to be so great that, in order to save them, He willed the death of His Son; and, on the other hand, seeing the love of the Son in wishing to die for us: in order to conform herself who was always and in all things united to the will of God to this excessive love of both the Father and the Son towards the human race, she also with her entire will offered, and consented to, the death of her Son, in order that we might be saved.[5]

St. Alphonsus Liguori, citing the authority of St. Anselm and St. Antoninus, takes this claim to an even more shocking level when he states that "if executioners had been wanting she herself would have crucified Him, in order to obey the Eternal Father Who willed His death for our salvation. If Abraham had such fortitude as to be ready to sacrifice with his own hands the life of his son, with far greater fortitude would Mary...have sacrificed the life of hers."[6]

What all of this underscores, as the Benedictine abbot Arnold of Bonneval (+1156) observes, is that "at that moment, Christ and Mary had but one single will, and both were equally offering a single holocaust to God: she with the blood of her heart; he with the blood of his body."[7] St. Anthony of Padua (+1231) points out, "Christ endured his Passion in the body that was nourished by the Virgin's milk."[8] And the French author Charles Peguy (+1914) says poetically, "She suffered in his head and in his side and in his four wounds."[9]

In the silent beholding between Mother and Son that transpired when they met on the road to Calvary, each experienced the gaze of the Father. Face to face with his mother, Jesus says in his heart: "Behold, the Lamb of God who takes away the sins of the world." To which the silent Mary responds: "Behold, I am the handmaid of the Lord."

Our Lady of Sorrows surrenders herself to such excruciating suffering in order to be in solidarity with us. We need suffering in our life. The writer Leon Bloy (+1917) famously stated that there are places in the heart that do not yet exist; suffering has to enter in for them to come to be.

Pope John Paul II taught that it is through suffering that we go beyond ourselves and come in contact with our transcendence.[10] Pope Benedict wrote that "the true measure of humanity is essentially determined in relationship to suffering and to the sufferer."[11]

Why? The twentieth-century Catholic philosopher Louis Lavelle helps us understand: "Suffering cuts through all the appearances behind which we hide, until it reaches the depths where the living self dwells.... It is suffering that deepens our consciousness, making it understanding and loving.... The real problem is not to find a way to anesthetize suffering, since that could only be done at the expense of consciousness itself. The problem is how to transfigure it."[12]

Father Julian Carron continues in this vein: "Even for people who live anesthetized lives, anesthetics have a limit because suffering and the wound are unavoidable. Grace enters through this suffering and this wound."[13]

When we find the courage to come to terms with the wounds in our lives, we see the face of one who first sympathized with our suffering—Our Lady of Sorrows: "When the apostles fled," St. Ambrose tells us, "Mary stood before the Cross and gazed tenderly on the wounds of her Son, because she was waiting, not for her Son's death, but for the salvation of the world."[14] That is, she was waiting for the salvation *of us*.

New Motherhood

Mary waits at the cross *as Mother*. St. Alphonsus Liguori relates that "Jesus, in…seeing the ardent desire of Mary to aid in the salvation of [humankind], … disposed it so that she, by the sacrifice and offering of the life of her Jesus, should cooperate in our salvation, and thus become the Mother of our souls."[15]

The universal dimension of the Blessed Virgin's motherhood was revealed only on Calvary, in Jesus' gift of a mother who thereby became our mother as well. In the words that Christ speaks to Mary and the Beloved Disciple—"Woman, behold, your son!… Behold, your mother!" (John 19:26, 27)—he establishes a new relationship of love between Mary and Christians. "The words of the dying Jesus," Pope John Paul II wrote, "actually show that his first intention was not to entrust his Mother to John, but to entrust the disciple to Mary and to give her a new maternal role."[16]

In this way, beneath the cross, "her vision would still be that of a mother giving birth."[17] Mary, the woman born to be the Mother of God, looks up at her Son, who was born to die. The words uttered by the Crucified become the Blessed Virgin's supreme consolation. They proclaim: "It is not over! Death will not have the last word. Malice will not put an end to your maternal vocation. You are still giving birth. From this day forward all generations will call you Blessed Mother."

The reason why the Mother of God can face what is utterly unbearable is because of the spiritual children she has yet to bear. The Benedictine abbot Rupert of Deutz extols Mary's new motherhood: "Because on Calvary the Blessed Virgin truly suffered the pangs of a woman in childbirth, and because in her Son's Passion she gave birth to the salvation of us all, she is clearly the Mother of us all."[18]

Our Lady of Compassion

At the Annunciation the angel announced that Mary would receive God in her own body, giving flesh to him. On Good Friday Mary once again receives the Word of God, as her divine Son is taken down from the cross and placed in her arms. Even in the sickening shadow of the cross, the power of the Most High continues to overshadow the Blessed Virgin Mary.

The Mother of God cradles in her arms all our failure, our desperation, our loneliness, our regret, our helplessness, our nothingness, our defeat. This terrible moment on Golgotha is a kind of second Epiphany. Like the magi, we have followed not a luminous star but the eclipse-blackened sun to this place of horror. Here we find the child with Mary his Mother. Here, as once did those three kings, we prostrate ourselves and do homage. And we open up the coffers of our empty, hurting hearts.

This, in fact, is the providential purpose of suffering. Pope John Paul II has told us that suffering conceals "a particular power *that draws a person interiorly close to Christ.*"[19]

As we draw close to Christ in our suffering, we receive Mary. Our crucified Savior has confided to us his Sorrowful Mother, with all her maternal closeness, in order to sustain us when we are overcome by the terrifying trials of life. Through Mary's compassionate presence at the cross, the passion that continues to play itself out in our life becomes more deeply human. St. Albert the Great (+1280) says that "as all the world is under obligation to Jesus for his Passion, so also are we under obligation to Our Lady for her compassion."[20] For Our Lady of Compassion fills us with the courage to face life's sufferings, certain in her secure embrace of divine providence.

Dionysius the Carthusian (+1471) asks: "If the Virgin felt with the bride and bridegroom of Cana the sorrow of their physical poverty and came to their aid, even without being asked, how much more will she have compassion on our spiritual neediness and offer assistance if she be called upon with faith? Yes, she offers assistance generously, even before she is asked."[21] "Mary is so endued with feelings of compassion," says St. Leo the Great, "that she not only deserves to be called merciful, but even mercy itself."[22]

In a unique, unrepeatable manner, the presence of Mary at Calvary instills *humanity* into a scene of total *inhumanity*. And the Blessed Mother can do this because she alone has in herself the purity that can bear *the darkness of faith*. In the face of devastating death, we need something bigger than life.

Consider Michelangelo's famous *Pieta*. In this sculpture Mary holds the dead body of Jesus on her lap. However, Michelangelo depicts the sorrowful Mother as being *younger* than her Son. Moreover, Mary's face is not in any way distraught, but rather her countenance is recollected and radiant with gentleness and holy resignation. And although the Blessed Mother's head is the same size as that of her Son, her *body* is much bigger. In fact, if the Madonna of the *Pieta* were to stand up, she would be nearly seven feet tall.

By these details the statue seems to proclaim: All you who are like the dead child in this woman's arms, who allow her to embrace you, Our Lady of Sorrows promises you youth, serenity, surrender, security, confidence, newness, another chance, life.

In giving us his mother to be our mother, Jesus begins to fulfill the great promise he uttered at the Last Supper: "I will not leave you orphaned" (John 14:18, *NAB*). And the matchless way that Mary "beholds" us changes the way that we look at ourselves. Origen (in the third century) wrote, "In other words, he said to her, 'This man is Jesus, whom you bore.' Indeed, when someone is perfect, 'it is no longer he that lives, but Christ lives in him' (cf. Gal 2:20); therefore when he speaks of [the Beloved Disciple] to Mary, he says, 'Behold your son,' that is, Jesus Christ."[23]

A Saving Love

Maureen and Skip, a young married couple from New York, decided after a six-year struggle with infertility to adopt a twenty-month-old orphan from Russia. The little boy's name was Seriozha.

The long flight home was a nightmare. Seriozha erupted in horrible tantrums; he flailed about, banged his head, bit his fingers, screamed. He would keep up that kind of hostile behavior for two agonizing years. Then, amazingly, Seriozha began to change and to make a secure attachment to his new family.

The doctor who helped with the adoption process confessed, "I spent a few years being frightened about this kid." But that was not the end of the story because, as she put it, "his parents fell in love with this child. I think they saw who he was."[24]

Our Lord from the cross gives us his mother to be our mother so that she will see who we really are. The gaze of Our Lady of Sorrow's love saves us from our savage and self-destructive ways.

George Bernanos, in *The Diary of a Country Priest*, wrote:

> The Virgin looks at us with eyes of a child; hers is the only truly childlike gaze which has ever rested upon our misfortunes.... It is a look of tender compassion, of sorrowful surprise, of some inconceivable innocence and concern for us that makes her younger than sin, younger than the race to which she belongs, and although Mother of God by the grace of God, Mother of the graces that flow from him, yet still the youngest daughter of mankind and our own companion and Mother.[25]

No wonder so many take refuge in Our Lady of Sorrows. Amadeus of Lausanne gives a kind of survey of those who do:

> There come to Mary's doors people beating their breasts, confessing their sins, and having received pardoned they return home with joy. There come also those who are sick in mind, weak in the head, the mad, the maniacs, the possessed, those who are led astray by nightly terrors, by some phantasma or by a genuine attack of the evil one, and they regain their health and receive the generosity of the divine gift. In the same way there draw near to her feet those whose hearts are bitter: the sad, the needy, the afflicted, the lonely, those tied up by debt and, most grievous of all, those living in dishonor and besmirched with the stain of ill-repute. The prayers of all these who cry out of whatever tribulation she gladly receives and, making supplication to her Son, in her pity she turns from them every evil. For just as wax melts at the touch of fire and as ice melts in the heat

of the sun, so the army of her foes perishes before her face and at her bidding nothing hostile stands.[26]

We long to share the certainty with which Bl. Henry Suso reveres the mystery of Our Lady of Sorrows:

> Some may rejoice in their innocence, others may be glad of their plentiful merits, let others exult in God's mercy shown to them without intermediaries; but you, my Mother, you are the only hope and solace of my life. When I completely despair of God and of myself, thinking of you, recalling you, my spirit comes alive again, as if out of the deepest darkness. You are my glorying, my well-being, my honor, and my life. Remember, loving Mother, that mothers are accustomed to cherish their ailing children with greater care, to sympathize more with them, and to give them a more constant attention …. My wounds are known to you, loving Mother. Do you visit your sick, raise up the dead.[27]

When Jesus entrusts his Sorrowful Mother to the Beloved Disciple, the disciple welcomes Mary into his home and "brings her into everything that makes up his inner life, that is to say into his human and Christian 'I',… establishing a profound communion of life with her."[28]

Perhaps the Prologue of the Gospel of John was the fruit of that "profound communion of life." Maybe, as some suggest, one day Mary told John, "In the beginning was my Son. My Son was in God's presence, and my Son was God. My Son was present to God in the beginning. Through my Son all things came into being, and apart from my Son nothing came to be. Whatever came to be in my Son found life."

chapter nine

THE ASSUMPTION
Sharing in the Mysteries of Heaven

FRIEND TOLD ME ABOUT A NIGHT HE VISITED WITH his four-year-old granddaughter. The two of them read together a book about the stars. When they finished the little girl suggested that they actually go outside and look at the stars. To their great luck, as they gazed into the sky, they saw a shooting star.

The little girl said, "Quick! Make a wish!" (for that is what you are supposed to do when you see a shooting star).

Some moments of silence ensued. And then the little girl asked, "Would you like me to tell you what I wished for?"

"If you want," replied the man.

The little girl said, "Grandpa, I wished that you would love me forever."

Looking into the splendor of the starry sky makes us long for the most splendid thing of all: to be loved forever by someone whose love makes all the difference in our lives. That is the essence of the Assumption. As we gaze into the heavens where the Mother of God has been taken up bodily, we are moved to ask for the unending gift of her love, which has already transformed our lives in the most dramatic ways.

St. Amadeus of Lausanne writes, "Every holy and reasonable soul, examining the secret mysteries of heaven, finds first after the Redeemer the woman blessed among women, full of grace. This Blessed Virgin, more brilliant than every light, lights up the whole world."[1]

The mystery of the Assumption is the promise that the relationship of love that we have experienced in an earthly way with the Blessed Virgin Mary will be ours forever. The Mother of God acts to fulfill our dearest wish even before we can make it.

Minutes after the Lord's ascension, after Christ's disciples stopped "gazing into heaven" (Acts 1:10), they began to miss Jesus' face. In their sorrow they searched each other's faces until they gazed upon that of the Blessed Virgin Mary. And then their sorrow ceased. For in the face of the Mother of God they recognized, perhaps for the first time, the face of God's Son.

Pope John Paul II, in his beautiful Marian catechesis entitled *Theotokos*, makes the point that, by Mary's flesh-and-blood presence among the community of believers, she became a living reminder to the disciples of Jesus' face.[2] So strong was the physical resemblance between Mother and Son that it served as a source of constant consolation for the post-Ascension Church.

It has been shown that, if one superimposes the miraculous image of the face of Our Lady of Guadalupe onto that of the face of the crucified Christ in the Shroud of Turin or that of the risen Jesus in the Divine Mercy image revealed to St. Faustina, the features match up, and the two faces become one. Such a wonder reconfirms what Pope John Paul II asserts: "The Holy Spirit has spurred the Christian faith onward in its discovery of Mary's face."[3] For in that face we see what John Paul calls "the living icon of the Father's mercy."[4]

"The face of Christ's Mother," the pope assures us, "will continue to be the sign of God's mercy and tenderness for humanity."[5] That is one reason why it is so important for Mary's face to be present in heaven now.

Mary's Dormition, Translation, and Tomb

One remarkable thing about Mary's last days on earth is how long they were in coming. When Christ from the cross confided his mother to the Beloved Disciple (see John 19:26–27), it suggested they would be together for some time. Ancient sacred authors agree that the Blessed Mother's "falling asleep" or dormition did not occur immediately after the Ascension. According to the *Revelations* of St. Bridget of Sweden, Mary lived in the world another fifteen years.

St. Amadeus of Lausanne points to two reasons for this:

> Why did Mary suffer separation from her Son? Why was her holy desire, hotter than fire, held back? Because that delay was no small comfort for Christ's disciples. That delay did not detract from the Mother, and it brought to the world the medicines of salvation. With wondrous goodness provision was made for the primitive Church which no longer saw God present in the flesh, that it might see his mother and be refreshed by the lovely sight.[6]

And:

> Mary suffers delay that she may advance, she advances
> through her perseverance. Perseverance, joined to love
> and work, creates fullness, brings forth perfection.[7]

This fact about Our Lady's delayed death moved Bishop Bossuet to comment: "Indeed, it would be almost truer to say that the Blessed Virgin's death, caused by Divine Love, was the *cessation* of a miracle than that it was itself miraculous; for the real miracle lay rather in her being able to live on earth for so long parted from her Beloved."[8] In that miracle is a mercy for us.

Why did the miracle cease? The contemporary poet Richard Hobbs (+1993), speaking in the voice of Jesus, gives a practical reply:

> But what would you have done to her
> if I had left her among you?
> You would have made her
> into an idol, a goddess;
> you would have fought to own her
> to give your party
> power over your brothers and sisters;
> you would have used her words,
> or her silences,
> to prove your own point of view;
> and you would have forgotten me.
> She would have ceased to be
> the mother of your unity,
> and she would have become
> a curiosity and a scandal,
> the source of divisions among you.[9]

St. Cyril of Alexandria says, "The death of her is the entrance to life, where we shall find citizenship with Christ; the death of her is the turning-point of transformation into a better life, far better than anything created."[10]

Tradition (relayed by St. Bridget, St. Alphonsus Liguori, and several earlier sources) holds that, some days before Mary's death, the Lord sent the Archangel Gabriel to her again, to announce the impending event. The Blessed Mother prepared for her departure, St. Bridget informs us, by visiting all the places where her Son had suffered. Speaking in the voice of Mary, St. Bridget recounts: "And when one day my mind was absorbed in admiring contemplation of divine charity, my soul was filled therein with such exultation that it could not contain itself, and my soul was loosed from the body."[11]

Bossuet says that Mary's dormition "was wrought simply by the gradual perfecting of her love, which...at last reached such perfection that an earthly body could no longer contain it.... Even as the lightest touch will make a ripe fruit drop from its stem, so was this perfect spirit gathered in one moment to its heavenly home, without effort or shock."[12] In this Bossuet follows St. Francis de Sales, who speaks of Mary's dying "in love for her Son Jesus."[13]

As the Mother of God falls asleep in death, "she sinks to the bottom of surprise."[14] For her Son is at her side, ready to carry her soul, like an infant wrapped in swaddling clothes, to heaven (an event portrayed in ancient sacred art). Doctor of the Church St. John of Damascus sings, "The one who mysteriously has entered within you, to take his flesh from your virginity, he it is who welcomes you, taking your immaculate soul in his hands, embracing you—a loving, dutiful Son."[15]

But this is only the beginning. St. Gregory of Tours (+594) tells us that, after Jesus withdrew to heaven with the soul of his mother, the apostles proceeded to lay Mary's body in a tomb, where they kept watch, awaiting the coming of the Lord. For they anticipated the miracle of Mary's bodily "translation" to heaven.

What reasons could they have had for expecting such a supernatural move?

Before all else is Our Lady's immaculate dignity. St. Thomas Aquinas tells us that the last curse common to man and woman is that they must return to dust, yet Mary was free from this curse.[16] Since Mary's virginal body is the all-holy dwelling place of God, says St. Germanus of Constantinople, the possibility of that body's dissolving into dust is foreign to it. It is not possible that the vessel that contained God himself should be held by a tomb made for the dead. Rather, he insists, it is altogether fitting that God should make Mary a sharer in his community of life.[17]

In fact, the tomb itself becomes a place of salvation. When, as St. John of Damascus sings, "Christ brings his tabernacle glorious [his Mother] to a greater sanctuary and to a holier tent [heaven],"[18] Mary's tomb becomes a kind of paradise. It remains a sacred place imbued with divine fragrance and grace, a wellspring of healing, and a source of every blessing for anyone who approaches it with faith.

The Glory of Mary

The day of Mary's assumption was an occasion of unique exultation for the inhabitants of heaven. For until the Mother of God arrived, something was missing from heaven. Rainer Maria Rilke addresses this in his poem about the Assumption:

> Who would have believed that before she came
> the vast heavens had been incomplete?

The resurrected Christ had taken His place,
but next to Him, for twenty-four years,
the seat was vacant....

But as her graceful figure
now joined the new blessed
and inconspicuously stood, light on light,
there broke from her being a glory
of such radiance that an angel, lit up by it
and blinded, cried: Who is she?
All were amazed. Then they saw how
God the Father above held back our Lord
so that the empty place, brushed
by fading twilight, seemed a small sorrow,
a trace of loneliness,
like something that He still endured, a remnant
of earthly time, a dried affliction.[19]

Bishop Bossuet says that one reason the angels rejoiced at the Assumption was that they were "delighted to behold" the beautiful "completion of the Mystery whose beginnings they first announced."[20] Through Mary's obedience at the Annunciation, the Blessed Virgin clothed the Eternal Word with human flesh. But in the mystery of the Assumption, St. Bernard remarks, the Eternal Word clothes Our Lady with his own power and mercy.[21] This in turn transforms the lives of the angels. As an Armenian hymn for the Feast of the Assumption expresses it, "Today the choirs of fiery spirits look upon our own nature, made of clay, and tremble."[22]

This marvel led the seventeenth-century Mexican nun and poet Sor Juana Inés de la Cruz to exclaim:

Crowned with glory and honor,
the deeds that brought Mary fame,
since they cannot be contained on earth,
send her riding out of this world.

As knight errant of the spheres
on a new adventure,
she finds the hidden treasure
sought by so many.[23]

Mary Assumed Into Heaven: Our Intercessor, Our Hope

However, the treasure Mary finds is not meant for her alone; it is intended for us through Mary's maternal intercession. Her words to Jesus at the wedding feast of Cana reveal that the Blessed Mother exists to be an intercessor for us before her Son (see John 2:1–5). In fact, the reason for our devotion to Mary, says Bishop Bossuet, is rooted in one all-important fact: Mary's "power" with our Lord *remains the same* as it ever was during his life on earth: Her sway with her Son has not diminished or changed in heaven. For, Bossuet observes, natural human feelings are raised and perfected in glory; they are not extinguished. Through the mystery of the Blessed Virgin Mary assumed into heaven, the human nature that Christ took on at his conception now actually speaks to him through her.[24]

Mary's maternal intercession takes the form of *mediation*. Pope John Paul II tells us that, as a Mother, Mary "*wishes the messianic power of her Son to be manifested,* that salvific power of his which is meant to help man in his misfortunes, to free him from the evil which in various forms and degrees weighs upon his life."[25] For "the Church's mystery...consists in generating people to a new and immortal life: This is her motherhood in the Holy Spirit.

And here Mary is not only the Model and Figure of the Church: She is much more. For, *'with maternal love she cooperates in the birth and development'* of the sons and daughters of Mother Church.... The Church *draws* abundantly from this cooperation, that is to say from the maternal mediation which is characteristic of Mary."[26]

Thus we live the mystery of the Assumption by venerating this dimension of Mary's motherhood, "which becomes man's inheritance; [it] is a gift: *a gift which Christ himself makes* personally to every individual."[27] This moves us to beg with the fifteenth-century spiritual author Jean Gerson, "O beautiful one, pray for us to your sweet Son before his throne, that he might give us himself as our reward."[28]

The mystery of the Assumption imbues us with a special confidence in the intercession of the Blessed Virgin Mary precisely because of Mary's new *closeness with God*. Thanks to the miracle of the Assumption, we have been given a new, unlimited way to experience the Blessed Mother's love! Pope Benedict XVI explains that, while Mary lived on this earth, the physical constraints of the world made it possible for her to be close to only a few people. But now, precisely because Mary is with God and in God, she is immensely close to each one of us. By the grace of the Assumption, Mary shares in the very closeness of God who is within us all.[29]

St. Andrew of Crete confirms this: "While living among us, only a tiny bit of our earth did possess you. Now that you ascended on high the entire world will clasp you to its bosom as the universal peace-maker between it and the offended God."[30]

Thanks to this mystery, says Bishop Bossuet, "we are actually bound to believe that we poor creatures may raise our desires even so high as to union with our Maker."[31] St. Germanus of Constantinople voices that desire: "Even though you departed, Mary, you did not separate yourself from the Christian people. You, the way leading to incorruptibility, did not distance yourself from this corruptible world; on the contrary, you remain close to those who call upon you. They who seek you faithfully do not fail to find you."[32]

How we crave this closeness! The renowned twentieth-century spiritual writer Monsignor Ronald A. Knox captures our longing in a striking image. He notes that the transformation of our material bodies—a transformation that we all look forward to one day—has been accomplished in the Blessed Virgin Mary. The coming of Christ has turned our hearts heavenward.

> And as the traveler, shading his eyes while he contemplates some long vista of scenery, searches about for a human figure that will give him the scale of those distant surroundings, so we, with dazzled eyes looking Godwards, identify and welcome one purely human figure, close to his throne. One ship has rounded the headland, one destiny is achieved, one human perfection exists. And as we watch it, we see God clearer, see God greater, through this masterpiece of his dealings with mankind.[33]

Mary's bodily presence in heaven, then, changes the way we face reality, with all its hurts and trials and sorrows. It is a change called *hope*. St. Amadeus of Lausanne says that the Blessed Mother, "entering upon the paths of justice" at her Assumption, "has left behind clear footprints for those coming after."[34] Through the Assumption of the Blessed Virgin Mary, writes Pope John Paul II, "hope is enriched with ever new reasons."[35]

Mary teaches Christian believers to look to the future with total abandonment to God because, assumed into heaven, she "communicates to them an ever new capacity to await God's future and to abandon themselves to the Lord's promises."[36] Filled with that holy abandonment, St. Hildebert of Fontenelle (+1133) exclaims, "You, O Lady, teach us to hope for far greater graces than we deserve, since you never cease to dispense graces far beyond our merits."[37]

The great sixteenth-century Dominican preacher Venerable Louis of Grenada makes the point that, of all the feasts in honor of the Blessed Virgin Mary, there is something truly distinctive about the Assumption. For all Mary's other feasts, however glorious, contain something of the vale of tears of this earth; they involve a mixture of sorrow and joy. But the feast of Mary's Assumption is a feast of "pure joy," and that is why it can properly be called "her" feast.[38] We are called to share in that joy, St. John of Damascus says, "our faces shining with Mary's radiance."[39]

Indeed, the face that gave so much comfort to the disciples after the Ascension continues to gaze upon the Church with love today. By that face that forever dwells with God, we see God more clearly. We trustingly await God's future with the new, blessed capacity given to us in the Assumption. After all, the mother's arms that once held the infant Jesus are now in heaven, opened wide, waiting to embrace us.

chapter ten

THE QUEENSHIP OF MARY
Increasing the Splendor of the Elect

THERE IS A STRIKING SCENE IN THE GOSPEL OF JOHN after our Lord miraculously feeds the five thousand with multiplied loaves and fishes. The people exclaim, "This is truly the prophet who is to come into the world." Whereupon Christ withdraws to the mountain alone, for he perceives that they are about to carry him off to make him their king (John 6:14–15).

Whenever we experience something supremely good, we want to "crown" it. That is, we try to make it last, taking the necessary measures to ensure it will stay, even to the point of letting it rule our lives.

The mystery of the Queenship of Mary can be understood through this human experience. The fourteenth-century Dominican mystic Bl. Henry Suso observes,

> When our heart is oppressed with grief and fear and can find no remedy for its suffering, we have no recourse but to look upward to the Queen of Heaven, the Virgin

> Mary.... How many sinners, after abandoning and
> denying their Lord, losing all hope, have found refuge in
> you, and, under your protection, returned to God's
> grace![1]

In this regard no one has to inform us about the historical coronation of the Blessed Virgin Mary; our heart knows well that
Mary dwells in heaven as a queen who lives to assist us in overcoming whatever afflicts or limits us. In fact, if God did not
crown Mary queen, we would beg heaven that he do so. The
goodness we have received from Our Lady's maternal mediation
is so profound that to love her without loving her as queen would
be to love her in a way that is lacking.

We cannot truly appreciate the countless graces we have
received from God without being thankful, and we cannot be sufficiently thankful without returning to the source of those graces.
Which leads us to the Mother of God, Queen of Heaven. For as
the renowned Dominican theologian St. Albert the Great says so
aptly, "The throne of grace is the Blessed Virgin Mary."[2]

Queen Because Mother

Mary's queenship is not something "added on" to her motherhood but is rather the glorious result of it. "When Mary became
the Mother of the Creator," writes St. John of Damascus, "she
truly became the queen of all creatures."[3] For, Arnold of Bonneval
states, "the Mother cannot be separated from the Son's dominion
and power,"[4] and that union with the Son of God's dominion is
the Mother of God's queenship. Just as the Blessed Virgin is destined to be the Mother of God, so too is she to be heaven's queen.
"From the moment when she conceived God in her womb," says
St. Bernardine of Siena, "she had...a certain jurisdiction and

authority over all the temporal processions of the Holy Spirit, so that no creature receives any grace of virtue except through the distribution of that grace by the Virgin Mary."[5]

This follows an eminent wisdom, noted by St. Louis de Montfort: "It is through the Blessed Virgin Mary that Jesus Christ came into the world; and it is also fitting that, through her, He should reign over the world."[6] Indeed, as St. Anthony of Padua explains, it could not be otherwise: "Truly the grace of the Blessed Virgin was greater than any other grace, for she and God the Father had the same Son, and thus she merited...to be crowned in heaven."[7]

The supreme beauty of Mary's queenship appears in her maternity. St. Thérèse of Lisieux, who lost her own mother when she was but a little girl, speaks from experience about this:

> We know very well that the Blessed Virgin is Queen of heaven and earth, but she is more Mother than Queen; I believe she'll increase the splendor of the elect very much. What the Blessed Virgin has more than we have is the privilege of not being able to sin, she was exempt from the stain of original sin; but on the other hand, she wasn't as fortunate as we are, since she didn't have a Blessed Virgin to love.[8]

Thus, as queen Mary has the power to "increase the splendor of the elect"; and as mother, the loving determination to make sure it happens. As Pope John Paul II pointed out: "Taken up into heavenly glory, Mary dedicates herself totally to the work of salvation in order to communicate to every living person the happiness granted to her. She is a Queen who gives all that she possesses, participating above all in the life and love of Christ."[9]

Queen of Our Salvation

The majesty of Mary saves us from the scandal of our sin. The twelfth-century Premonstratensian Philip of Harveng assures us of this:

> The Virgin has a certain affectionate feeling of deeper goodwill toward those whom she sees to be in need of the patronage of someone stronger than themselves; that is, those...who are so oppressed by the weight [of their sins] that they cannot make progress. The Virgin loves...to move the weak toward stronger things with loving goodwill.[10]

As queen the Blessed Mother exercises a special sovereign authority toward those who otherwise would be lost. St. Thomas Aquinas teaches, "Through Mary's intercession, many souls are in paradise who would not be there had she not interceded for them, for God has entrusted her with the keys and treasures of the heavenly Kingdom."[11] Even more, Mary the Queen, "by the support of her merits,... restores the repentant to the level of grace they had lost," according to St. Albert the Great.[12]

Paul the Deacon adjures us for this reason not to become blackmailed by our evil: "[N]o matter how horrible our [spiritual] weakness, we must never despair of her mercy, as long as we are willing to accuse ourselves in her sight and beg for her intercession with a repentant heart. There is no doubt that we will experience her help, for many are her mercies, and great mercy is given to all who call upon her."[13]

United with Mary, the awareness of our own shame moves us all the more to claim her maternal compassion. "The more you see yourselves as guilty before the majesty of God," writes the tenth-century bishop Fulbert of Chartres, "the more you should look to the Mother of the Lord, for she is full of mercy. ... [Y]ou may hope for forgiveness from him and from his Mother."[14]

The Queenship of Mary bestows upon us a particular intimacy with the Blessed Virgin. As our queen, says St. Peter Canisius (+1597), Mary "constitutes our protection; she keeps us close to Christ, and she faithfully takes the matter of our salvation into her charge."[15] And as St. Louis de Montfort notes, if Mary "wills to come and take up her abode in you, in order to receive her Son, she can do so by reason of the sovereignty she possesses over the hearts of people."[16]

Mary's coronation in heaven guarantees her closeness in our earthly afflictions. The great sixth-century hymnographer Romanos the Melodist has the Queen of Heaven speak: "[N]o more sadness, because I have brought joy to the world. For it is to destroy the kingdom of sorrow that I have come into the world: I, full of grace."[17] G.K. Chesterton expresses the same conviction in one of his poems: "That life that was Mary's shall guard us."[18]

To live the mystery of the Queenship of Mary is to pray confidently with Eadmer of Canterbury (+1130): "Having become the glorious Queen of heaven, you might rule over all things… and prepare for a fallen world the entry into recovery and the prize of eternal life."[19]

This prize of eternal life is the "crown" that Christ promises to his faithful followers: "Blessed is the man who endures trial, for when he has stood the test he will receive the crown of life which God has promised to those who love him" (James 1:12). The Blessed Mother already wears that crown, and it is her joy and delight to share her royal dignity with all who call upon her in trust. And so we beg with the abbot of Cluny Peter the Venerable (+1156), "Look down, and melt away our crime, O Mistress of the world,"[20] so that we, like you, may "obtain the unfading crown of glory" (1 Peter 5:4).

chapter eleven

THE IMMACULATE HEART OF MARY
Knowing the Mother of God by Heart

O N JANUARY 1, 1996, POPE JOHN PAUL II ELEVATED THE liturgical celebration of the Immaculate Heart of Mary from an optional memorial to an obligatory memorial. This shift signaled to the Church that there is something essential and indispensable about the Immaculate Heart of Mary for the life of faith.

Why is Mary's heart—or any heart—important?

The Church's Understanding of Heart

The *Catechism of the Catholic Church* teaches that the "heart" is our hidden center, the dwelling-place of our "I," the locus of truth where we choose life or death—the place of encounter with the relationship with the Infinite *that we are* (*CCC*, 2563). The sad fact is that, for various reasons—our fallenness, our actual sins, the adverse influence of the world, and so on—many of us do not live according to our heart.

For the human heart exists in a state of profound *expectation*, longing for the answers to life's big questions: Why do I exist?

What is the meaning of life? What is my purpose in life? Why is there suffering in the world, and how am I supposed to deal with it? Is happiness real, and if so, what is the key to my happiness? These questions are daunting, and when the answers to them are not immediately apparent, the questions become overwhelming. We would prefer to ignore them rather than be tormented by them. We even have an expression for this—we speak of "losing heart."

Losing our zest for life happens when we "reduce" our heart. This consists in attempting to compromise the heart's urgent needs. We adopt an "anesthetized" mode of living by which we keep life's big questions at bay. We try to content ourselves with what is mediocre—with creature comforts, convenience, superficial interests, what is "safe," passing pleasures, indulgences, concessions, and so on. In place of true, deep satisfaction, we settle for mere complacency.

The remarkable thing, though, is that the human heart *unfailingly knows* if what it is offered is sufficient for its happiness; no one needs to educate the heart about what is enough for it. (You know this from your own experience.) When something does not measure up to the expectation of our heart, we sense it automatically. It is an experience called *disappointment*, and the very existence of disappointment *proves* that the human heart is made for Something More (no matter how much we try to deny it). Even if we do not know *what* that Something More is, we know *that* that Something More is.

Thus the Lord speaks to us through the prophet Jeremiah: "Then you will call upon me and come and pray to me, and I will hear you. You will seek me and find me; when you seek me with all your heart" (Jeremiah 29:12–13).

The *totality* that we are searching for is to be found only in God, and we can find it only if we seek God "with *all* our heart." Therefore we need someone to restore the heart that we have lost. The Church exists to give us back our heart. And the Church gives us our heart in the same manner that the eternal Father gives his incarnate Son his human heart: through the Blessed Virgin Mary.

Mary's Heart as the Beginning

"So great was the love of Mary," explains St. Augustine, "that it conquered the omnipotent God."[1] That is to say, the very heart that the Father gave Mary *won him over!* So, too, the Son. Pope John Paul II wrote that "the love that Christ wanted to pour forth in the world was kindled and burned first of all in his Mother's heart."[2] It moves Jesus, says the Church's foremost promoter of devotion to the Immaculate Heart of Mary, St. John Eudes, to pour "into the heart of his Mother the plenitude of the treasures of wisdom and knowledge that are hid in his own heart."[3]

From that plenitude everything proceeds. Hugo Rahner tells us, "Everything has its beginning in the heart of Mary, and in her womb.... In the midst of her heart, eternity entered time."[4]

The Church rejoices in the fact that Mary conceived Jesus in her heart before conceiving him in her womb. St. Augustine even suggests that "Mary's loving motherhood would indeed have profited little, had she not first conceived Christ in her heart, and only then in her womb."[5]

That beginning, that method, has not changed for us. God gives us the Immaculate Heart of Mary to venerate and to love so that eternity will enter our concrete here and now and transform it. How crucial it is for us then to be one with the Immaculate

Heart of Mary and to live the mystery of this inestimable gift. We are offered Mary's Immaculate Heart in the liturgy so that we will "take heart."

Conformity With the Immaculate Heart of Mary

Into the heart of Mary came the Holy Spirit, "with a fullness that filled it to human capacity."[6] How our hearts languish when they fail to encounter what will fill them to their capacity. What God's Spirit does in the heart of Mary he wills to do in our own hearts *through* Mary, so that we will also experience that fullness. St. Louis de Montfort assures us:

> This Mother of fair love will remove from your heart all scruples, and every taint of slavish and disordered fear. She will open your heart and make it big and generous; so that you may run in the way of the commandments of her Son, with the holy liberty of the children of God, and be given a share of that pure love of which she is the treasurer.… [Y]ou will … be led… by pure love of Him Who is love. You will look upon Him as your own good Father, Whom you will endeavor to please at all times, and with Whom you will speak confidently, as a child with his loving father.…
>
> The Blessed Virgin will fill you with great confidence in God and in herself. She will do so because you no longer approach Jesus Christ by your own self, but always through this good Mother; because, since you have given her all your merits, graces and satisfactions, to be disposed of as she wishes, she in turn gives you her virtues and clothes you with her merits.[7]

Why can Mary's Immaculate Heart accomplish this? Because, as the esteemed theologian and preacher Bossuet points out, God in his wonderful justice fills the Blessed Virgin's heart "with an affection far beyond that of mere nature, and reaching even to the very highest degree of grace; so that she might have for her Son feelings that should be at the same time fit for a mother of God, and worthy of a God-man."[8]

This is why St. Louis de Montfort implores: "Beg this good Mother to lend you her heart, that you may have a dwelling wherein to receive Him with her dispositions."[9] The twelfth-century abbot Philip of Harveng imagines the Blessed Virgin Mary saying to us,

> When I lead you forth out of the darkness of ignorance, as if giving birth to you; when with zeal and labor I guide you to the light of truth and knowledge; when, with loving concern, I teach you the perfect rules of life, what is it I am doing if not taking the place of a mother and training you in conformity with my heart?[10]

This overwhelming mercy moves us to exclaim with St. John Eudes: "Take away the heart of Mary, the true sun of the Christian world, and what would be left? Without Mary's radiance, nothing is left but enveloping darkness, the shadow of death and the frightful night of the grave."[11]

In Love With Jesus

United with the Immaculate Heart of Mary, we can love Jesus Christ with the love that he deserves (a love that we cannot stir up or invent on our own). At the same time our conformity with the Immaculate Heart of Mary is what gives us access to the treasures of Christ's Sacred Heart. St. Peter Julian Eymard states that "those who would know the intimate secrets of Divine Love and the hidden virtues of Jesus' Divinity must study them in the transparent mirror of the Immaculate Heart of Mary."[12] Or as Dominican Fr. Antonin Sertillanges expresses succinctly and profoundly, "Praying through Mary is aiming at Jesus in her heart."[13]

By giving ourselves over to the Immaculate Heart of Mary in this way, we gain a fuller share in the victory Christ won for us on the cross. For, St. John Eudes tells us, "the Heart of the Glorious Virgin contributed to the work of our Redemption, because Jesus Christ…is the fruit of her Heart."[14] And, St. Bonaventure adds, "those wounds which were scattered over the body of Our Lord were all united in the single Heart of Mary."[15]

A powerful story related in the seventh book of St. Bridget of Sweden's *Revelations* reveals what happens when we let ourselves be carried away by the love of the Immaculate Heart of Mary. St. Bridget is invited to be present at a heavenly tribunal, at which the devil and the Virgin Mary contend for the soul of an extremely wicked man who has died. The devil cries out to the Judge, Jesus Christ,

> Hearken, O most almighty Judge! I complain in your sight about a woman who is both my Lady [!!] and your Mother and whom you love so much that you have given to her power over heaven and earth and over all of us demons of hell. She has indeed done me an injustice regarding that soul which now stands here…. I ought to have taken it to myself…. [T]hat woman, your Mother, seized this soul with her own hands, almost before it exited from the man's mouth.

The Blessed Mother rebuts,

> I tell you...that it was my business, rather than yours, to present that soul before God.... For while this soul was in the body it had a great love for me, and in its heart frequently pondered the fact that God had deigned to make me his mother and that he willed to exalt me on high above all created things. As a result he began to love God with such great charity that in his heart he used to say this: "I so rejoice because God holds the Virgin Mary his Mother most dear above all things, that there is in the world no creature and no bodily delight that I would take in exchange for that joy. And if it were possible that God could remove her, in the smallest point, from that dignity in which she stands, I would rather choose for myself, in exchange, eternal torture in the depth of hell...." Therefore, O devil, see now with what sort of will he passed away.
>
> After a lengthy discussion the devil concluded with loud howling, clamoring like a maniac, "Woe is me. I have not one word to say; for my tongue has been cut off at the root!"
>
> And an angel informed him: "His mother did this with her continual prayers and her labor; for she loved his soul with her whole heart. Therefore, for the sake of her love, it pleased God to pardon all the venial sins that he committed from his infancy right up to his death; and therefore your tongue is said to have lost its strength."[16]

Mindfulness of the inestimable mystery of the Immaculate Heart of Mary moves us to join in the beautiful "Prayer for the Heart of a Child" composed by the French Jesuit theologian Fr. R.P. Leonce de Grandmaison (+1927):

> Holy Mary, Mother of God,
> preserve in me the heart of a child,
> pure and transparent as a spring.
> Obtain for me a simple heart
> that does not brood over sorrows;
> a heart generous in giving itself,
> quick to feel compassion;
> a faithful, generous heart
> that forgets no favor
> and holds no grudge.
> Give me a humble, gentle heart,
> loving without asking any return;
> a great indomitable heart
> that no ingratitude can close,
> no indifference can weary;
> a heart tortured by its desire
> for the glory of Jesus Christ:
> pierced by His love
> with a wound that will heal
> only in heaven.[17]

chapter twelve

THE HOLY NAME OF MARY
Doing What the Angels Do

HE WORLD BEGINS TO CHANGE WHEN AN ANGEL SPEAKS a name: "Hail Mary!"

The *Catechism of the Catholic Church* teaches, "Everyone's name is sacred. The name is the icon of the person. It demands respect as a sign of the dignity of the one who bears it" (*CCC*, 2158). Even more, "A name expresses a person's essence and identity and the meaning of this person's life. To disclose one's name is to make oneself known to others; in a way it is to hand oneself over by becoming accessible, capable of being known more intimately and addressed personally" (*CCC*, 203).

Thus we are awestruck and humbled before a Scripture verse that we might otherwise mistake as merely informational: "and the virgin's name was Mary" (Luke 1:27). We do not know the name of the woman at the well, we do not know the name of the widow in the temple, we do not know the name of the woman with a hemorrhage, we do not know the name of the adulterous woman and of many other women in the Gospels. But from the very beginning God insists on revealing to us the name of his mother.

God deliberately confides to us Mary's name so as to make the Blessed Virgin more accessible to us, to enable us to address her personally and know her intimately, and to give us an entree to the very meaning of her life. The honor of knowing and speaking the name of Mary is a divine privilege beyond all measure.

St. Thomas Aquinas (along with many other theological authors) points out that "Mary means '*star of the sea*,' for as mariners are guided to port by the ocean star, so Christians attain to glory through Mary's maternal intercession."[1] This from the man whose first words as a child were *Ave Maria*.

The fifteenth-century French theologian Jean Gerson, speaking in Our Lady's voice, elaborates on the significance of Mary's name: "Light spreads out because of its natural generosity, so that it is rightly called 'illuminatrix.' This, then, is the meaning of my own name, 'Mary.' Thus, as Mary, I am called etymologically 'Star of the Sea,' because my role is to illuminate."[2]

With this understanding of Our Lady's name, St. John Eudes directs us,

> Return thanks to the Father of Light and supplicate him to make you feel the effects of that precious name, Mary, which not only signifies "enlightened" but also "enlightener" and "enlightening." Pray Our Lady of Light to give you a share in that radiance that you may know the infinite goodness of God, in order to love him; the frightful horror of sin, in order to hate it; the vanity of the things of this world, in order to despise them, and the abyss of your own nothingness, that you may humble yourself.[3]

Mystical writers seem caught up in a kind of competition in making extravagant claims about the Blessed Mother's name. St. Louis de Montfort asserts that "the most holy name of Mary was sent from heaven from the adorable heart of the Most Holy Trinity, where it was cherished from all eternity. It was carried to earth by the Archangel Gabriel, who announced it to St. Joachim and St. Anne. This blessed name is a marvelous treasure containing within itself all riches."[4] And the Jesuit doctor of the Church St. Peter Canisius states: "After the most holy and adorable Name of Jesus, there is no name more glorious or more powerful than the name of Mary. At the mention of this name, the angels rejoice and the devils tremble; through the invocation of this name, sinners obtain grace and pardon."[5]

Salvation and Mary's Name

However, the true greatness of the Holy Name of Mary is its instrumentality in our salvation. "Just as the salvation of the world began with the Hail Mary," explains St. Louis de Montfort, "so the salvation of each individual is bound up with it." For just as the utterance of this name "brought to a dry and barren world the Fruit of Life," so, too, will reverently pronouncing the Holy Name of Mary in prayer "cause the Word of God to take root in the soul and bring forth Jesus, the Fruit of Life.... The Hail Mary is a heavenly dew which waters the earth of our soul and makes it bear its fruit in due season."[6]

We recognize our need for salvation in the everyday experiences of our powerlessness and helplessness. We require something that enables us to escape from our own inability. In our yearning for salvation, we are looking for complete fulfillment and satisfaction, for total meaning, for the answer to the ultimate questions that plague us. God chooses to give us that answer through a virgin whom we can call by name.

William of Saint-Thierry asks, "O Lord, what else is your salvation but receiving from you the gift of loving you or being loved by you?"[7] When we say the name of Mary in faith, we receive the unsurpassable gift of being loved by God. Bl. Henry Suso exults, "When I pronounce the name of Mary, I feel myself inflamed with such love and joy, that between the tears and happiness with which I pronounce this beautiful name, I feel as though my heart might leave my breast!"[8]

Pope Benedict XVI points to this love as the hallmark of salvation: "When someone has the experience of a great love in his life, this is a moment of 'redemption' which gives a new meaning to his life.... Salvation consists, 'not in being immersed in namelessness,' but rather in the satisfaction in seeing God's face that will be granted to us."[9] The Holy Name of Mary rescues us from the abyss of namelessness.

No wonder then that saints through the centuries extol the salvific efficacy of Mary's name:

> St. John of Damascus writes, "The very name of the Mother of God contains the whole mystery of the economy of the Incarnation."[10]

> Richard of St. Lawrence declares, "There is no other name, after 'Jesus,' from which so much salvation is poured forth."[11]

> St. Ephrem the Syrian adds, "The name of Mary is the key of the gates of Heaven."[12]

And St. Ambrose exclaims: "Your name, O Mary, is a precious ointment, which breathes forth the odor of Divine grace. Let this ointment of salvation enter the inmost recesses of our souls."[13]

The Devil's Dread

Of the twelve steps that comprise the satanic pact, step number four is that of rejecting the Virgin Mary. Satanists would not go to such extremes in renouncing the Blessed Virgin Mary in the ritual of diabolical initiation if the might of the Mother of God were not real.

The mere utterance of Mary's name scares hell to hell. The Venerable Thomas à Kempis wrote that "the devils fear the Queen of heaven to such a degree, that only on hearing her great name pronounced, they fly from him who does so as from a burning fire."[14] St. Bonaventure says that human beings "do not fear a powerful hostile army as the powers of hell fear the name and protection of Mary." [15]

But that is not all. St. Louis de Montfort tells us that the very devils in hell, while fearing Mary, show her respect.[16] In a revelation to St. Bridget, Our Lady explained how "all the devils venerate and fear her name to such a degree, that on hearing it they immediately loosen the claws with which they hold the soul captive." In fact, Our Lady continued, "there is not on earth a sinner, however devoid he may be of the love of God, from whom the devil is not obliged immediately to fly, if he invokes her holy name with a determination to repent."[17] St. Bonaventure adds, "As wax melts before fire, so do the devils lose their power against those souls who remember the name of Mary and devoutly invoke it."[18]

Conversely, the Blessed Virgin revealed to St. Bridget that, "in the same way as the rebel angels fly from sinners who invoke the name of Mary, so also do the good angels approach nearer to just souls who pronounce her name with devotion."[19] Thus Thomas à Kempis instructs us:

> If the malignant one attacks you and hinders your prayer, pay him no heed, increase your praying and praising, but even more, invoke with greater intensity the name of Mary. Salute Mary, think Mary, honor Mary, lean on Mary, commend yourself to Mary and repeat the name of Mary. If you know and practice this method, the devil will fly away from you and you will become proficient in the spiritual life.[20]

Invoking the Holy Name of Mary

All this leads St. Alphonsus Liguori to beg, "Grant, O Lady, that we may often remember to name you with love and confidence; for this practice either shows the possession of divine grace, or else is a pledge that we shall soon recover it."[21] St. Bonaventure confesses, "Your name, O Mary, cannot be pronounced without bringing some grace to him who does so devoutly."[22] This is confirmed by St. Louis de Montfort:

> We know from experience that those who show positive signs of being among the elect appreciate and love the Hail Mary, and are always glad to say it. The closer they are to God, the more they love this prayer.... [T]he frequent thought and loving invocation of Mary is a sure indication that the soul [is] not estranged from God by sin.[23]

The benefits of the Holy Name of Mary go beyond even our inabilities. Bl. Raymond Jordano the Unlearned, the medieval abbot of Celles, says that "however hardened and diffident a heart may be, the name of this most Blessed Virgin has such efficacy, that if it is only pronounced, that heart will be wonderfully softened."[24] This point is stressed as well by the eleventh-century spiritual writer and close friend of St. Anselm, Eadmer of Canterbury: "If the name of [Mary] is invoked, even if the merits of the one who invokes her do not earn him a hearing, nevertheless her merits will intercede and he will be heard."[25]

A powerful example of this mystery can be found in the story of Jacques Fesch. Born in 1930 of a privileged Parisian family, Jacques at age twenty-four had grown bored and restless. He tired of the well-paying job that his father had arranged for him at his bank. Instead Jacques sailed boats, rode horses, and drove fast cars. He fathered two illegitimate children. Still discontent and conceiving a grandiose scheme to start a new life in the South Pacific, Jacques decided to rob a currency dealer not far from the Paris Stock Exchange.

During the evening rush hour on February 24, 1954, Jacques held up gold dealer Alexandre Silberstein at gunpoint. He grabbed 300,000 francs and ran. But not far. Jacques was pursued by Silberstein and a crowd. A thirty-five-year-old police officer, Jean Vergne, with his gun drawn, ordered Jacques to desist. Jacques Fesch pulled out his gun and fired three times, killing the policeman.

Arrested and imprisoned, the remorseless Jacques said to the prison chaplain, "I've got no faith. No need to trouble yourself about me."

But then Jacques met a Dominican priest and a Benedictine brother, and their friendship led him to a dramatic conversion. At the heart of that conversion, a profound love for the Blessed Virgin Mary was born. In his prison journal Jacques wrote: "O Mary! blessed name that I love and venerate from the depths of my being! I attest this from my own experience: when a heart has received from heaven the precious gift of having recourse to Mary in its sorrows, dangers, and trials, this heart finds peace, rest, blessedness."[26]

Sentenced to execution for his crime, Jacques mounted the scaffold on October 1, 1957. Moments before the blade of the guillotine fell, he spoke his last words: "Holy Virgin, have pity on me!" Jacques Fesch's cause for beatification is underway.[27]

With unfaltering confidence St. Bernard exhorts us, "If the winds of temptations surge, if you run aground on the shoals of troubles, call upon Mary. If you are tossed by the winds of pride or ambition or detraction or jealousy, call upon Mary. In dangers, in straits, in perplexity, call upon Mary. Let her name be always in your mouth and in your heart."[28]

Doing What the Angels Do

St. Louis de Montfort says that

> [E]very day, from one end of the earth to the other, in the highest heaven and in the lowest abyss, all things preach, all things proclaim the wondrous Virgin Mary. The nine choirs of angels, men and women of every age, rank and religion, both good and evil, even the very devils themselves are compelled by the force of truth, willingly or unwillingly, to call her blessed.[29]

According to St. Bonaventure, all the angels in heaven unceasingly call out to her: "Holy, holy, holy Mary, Virgin Mother of God." They greet her countless times each day with the angelic greeting, "Hail, Mary," while prostrating themselves before her, begging her as a favor to honor them with one of her requests.[30]

In obedience we happily do what the angels do.

The true magnificence of Mary's name shines through the words of Bl. Henry Suso: "O Mary, what must you yourself be, since your very name is so loving and gracious?"[31]

chapter thirteen

OUR LADY OF THE ROSARY
Contemplating With Mary the Face of Christ

*I*N HIS BOOK *THE SECRET OF THE ROSARY*, ST. LOUIS DE Montfort relates the legend of how St. Dominic received the rosary from the Blessed Virgin Mary. The future founder of the Order of Preachers was beset with sorrow when a heretical sect resisted his efforts to convert it to Christianity. Dominic withdrew into a forest, where he prayed unceasingly for three nights and days.

Our Lady then appeared to the saintly preacher and asked him, "Dear Dominic, do you know which weapon the Blessed Trinity wants to use to reform the world?"

St. Dominic replied, "Oh, my Lady, you know far better than I do, because next to your Son Jesus Christ, you have always been the chief instrument of our salvation."

To this the Mother of God responded, "I want you to know that, in this kind of warfare, the battering ram has always been the angelic psalter, which is the foundation stone of the New Testament. Therefore if you want to reach these hardened souls and win them over to God, preach my psalter."[1] Mary's "psalter" is the rosary.

This pious lore brings to light how hard evangelization is. Dominic discovered that, in order to convert others, a mere *discourse* was not enough; he needed something more. The story makes it plain that what Dominic required was a reliving of the *saving events* of Jesus Christ. After all, being Christian, as Pope Benedict XVI teaches, is not the result of a lofty idea but the encounter with an *event*, a Person.[2] And Dominic needed that event to be entrusted to him by the Mother of God, Our Lady of the Rosary. That way what he preached to the heretics would not be the product of his thought, his understanding, or his ingenuity but rather would be the fruit of Mary's womb.

What Is the Rosary?

One of the most comprehensive and compelling treatises on the rosary is Pope John Paul II's apostolic letter entitled *Rosarium Virginis Mariae* (On the Most Holy Rosary). The letter will serve as our main guide through this chapter. (The numbers in parentheses refer to the paragraphs of the document.)

The rosary is an amazing compendium of the gospel that contains its depth and its saving message and force in all their entirety (1). Through our praying of the rosary, the principal events of the life of Jesus Christ are reproposed to us. They pass before the eyes of our soul, putting us in living communion with Jesus through the heart of Mary (2).

There is great wisdom in this. Recall the Old Testament story of the Exodus. After the Hebrew people had been safely led out of the slavery of Egypt and brought to the sacred summit of Mount Sinai, they were afraid to be before the great God who had saved them. They took up a position at a distance and said to Moses, "You speak to us, and we will hear; but let not God speak to us, lest we die" (Exodus 20:19). We best face the redemptive moments of our life accompanied by one whom God has chosen. For the Israelites it was Moses, and for us it is Mary.

In a unique way the rosary immerses us in the mysteries of our Redeemer's life. By so doing the rosary ensures that what Christ has done for us "is profoundly assimilated, and shapes our existence" (13).

In the first encyclical of Pope John Paul II, entitled *Redemptor Hominis* (*The Redeemer of Man*), the pontiff writes that anyone who wishes

> to understand himself thoroughly—and not just in accordance with immediate, partial, often superficial, and even illusory standards and measures of his being— must with his unrest, uncertainty, and even his weakness and sinfulness, with his life and death, draw near to Christ. He must, so to speak, enter into him with all his own self, he must "appropriate" and assimilate the whole of the reality of the Incarnation and Redemption in order to find himself.[3]

This indispensable process of drawing near to Jesus, appropriating and assimilating the reality of Christ, happens to us through the rosary. By our praying of the rosary, "we set out on a path of assimilation meant to help us enter more deeply into the life of Christ" (33).

In the experience of uniting us personally to the mysteries of our Savior's life, the rosary displays a remarkable sensitivity to our human needs—to the way we grow and learn and mature. For in the rosary "God communicates himself to us respecting our human nature and its vital rhythms…. The Rosary does indeed 'mark the rhythm of human life,' bringing it into harmony with the 'rhythm' of God's own life" (27, 25). The rosary's re-presentation of the events of Christ's life "bring[s] to mind what is essential and… awaken[s] in the soul a thirst for a knowledge of Christ continually" (24).

How we need in our life a "path of…increasing knowledge" of Christ (17) that is at the same time a sure "path of contemplation" (38). The rosary tells us again and again who we are and what we must do to be ourselves. The mysteries of the rosary shed light on the mystery of being human, bringing us face to face with the true image of the human person (25). "The Rosary helps us to be conformed ever more closely to Christ" (26). And in that conformity, as the rosary takes us "to the very heart of Christian life" (3), we find the meaning of life.

The "inner logic of the Incarnation" is that God in his Son made flesh wanted to take on human features, so that through Jesus' bodily reality we would be "led into contact with the mystery of his divinity" (29). Bl. Columba Marmion once commented that "all the holiness God has destined for our souls has been placed in the humanity of Christ, and it is from this source that we must draw."[4] In order to draw from this source, we do well to go to the one responsible for giving Jesus his humanity: Mary, the Mother of God. That is what we do in the rosary.

In short the rosary is the "true doorway to the depths of the Heart of Christ" (19). For this reason the act of praying the rosary "is not a matter of recalling information"—rather, as Pope John Paul II insists, it is a matter of "*allowing God to speak*" (30). Thus, "[t]o understand the Rosary, one has to enter into the psychological dynamic proper to love" (26), and to do this we turn to the one who loved Jesus best: Mary, the Mother of God, who is Our Lady of the Rosary.

The Face of Christ

Those who pray the rosary with all their heart know from experience that the rosary is an "outpouring of...love" (26). What evokes love in us like nothing else is the face of the beloved gazing at us. The rosary intends to be just that.

"The Rosary is one of the traditional paths of Christian prayer directed to the contemplation of Christ's face" (18). In fact, if we did not have the gift of the rosary in our life, we would search for a way to fix on Christ's face. In God's divine providence we do not need to invent this way, for "[w]ith the Rosary, the Christian people *sits at the school of Mary* and is led to contemplate the beauty on the face of Christ and to experience the depths of his love.... To recite the Rosary is nothing other than to *contemplate with Mary the face of Christ*" (1, 3).

The love poured out to us in the rosary orients us to both heaven and earth. For in contemplating Christ's face in the rosary, "we become open to receiving the mystery of Trinitarian life" (9), while at the same time "the Rosary leads to an encounter with Christ in his mysteries and so cannot fail to draw attention to the face of Christ in others, especially in the most afflicted" (40). And since "[n]o one has ever devoted himself to the contemplation of the face of Christ as faithfully as Mary" (10), Our Lady's role in our contemplating of Christ's face remains vital.

United With Mary, Who Prays With Us and for Us

Pope John Paul II revered the rosary as "an echo of the prayer of Mary, her perennial *Magnificat* for the work of the redemptive

Incarnation which began in her virginal womb" (1). What could be better than to be caught up in Our Lady's "perennial *Magnificat*"? For here is the fact: "Never as in the Rosary do the life of Jesus and that of Mary appear so deeply joined" (15).

And we want to share that union. "In the spiritual journey of the Rosary,…this demanding ideal of being conformed to [Christ] is pursued through an association which could be described in terms of friendship" (15). As we recite the rosary united with Mary, the Mother of God intercedes for us before the Father and before the Son born of her womb, praying with us and for us (16).

But why do we need this association? Why not simply pray on our own?

"[N]o one knows Christ better than Mary; no one can introduce us to a profound knowledge of his mystery better than his Mother" (14). Msgr. Romano Guardini explains:

> The essence of the rosary is a steady incitement to holy sympathy. If a person becomes very important to us, we are happy to meet someone who is attached to him. We see his image mirrored in another life and we see it anew. Our eyes meet two eyes that also love and see. Those eyes add their range of vision to ours, and our gaze may now go beyond the narrowness of our own ego and embrace the beloved being, previously seen only from one side. The joys that the other person experienced, and also the pains he suffered, become so many strings whose vibrations draw from our heart new notes, new understanding, and new responses.[5]

In other words, a most profound grace comes to us through the "method" of the rosary: "Contemplating the scenes of the Rosary in union with Mary is a means of learning from her to 'read' Christ, to discover his secrets and to understand his message.... It is not just a question of learning what he taught but of *'learning him'*" (14).

Pope John Paul II says that what comprised Mary's "rosary" were the events of Jesus' life that were so impressed upon her heart and that "she recited uninterruptedly throughout her earthly life" (11). As we said, the rosary is a path of contemplation, and "Mary's contemplation is above all *a remembering*" (13). "Remembrance" in this sense is a *making present* of the saving events of God in history. "To 'remember'...in a spirit of faith and love is to be open to the grace which Christ won for us by the mysteries of his life, death and resurrection" (13).

We want to be one with Mary's contemplating or remembering, so that the saving events of Christ's life will never stop acting in our life. We don't want the monumental events of our salvation to become abstractions, to turn into dead relics. We want those events to keep happening in our life, generating us, renewing us, and fortifying us every moment of our days. As the twentieth-century theologian Fr. Hans Urs von Balthasar explains:

> In recent Marian apparitions the rosary has played a part: it has happened that Mary has fingered the beads along with those praying the rosary. Why should this be?... So that it is from her point of view, from her memory that we should look at the mysteries of Jesus' life, and thereby at those of the Trinitarian embodiment of salvation. Our eyes are bleary and dull: if you will forgive the

metaphor, we must put on Mary's spectacles in order to see exactly.[6]

And "As we contemplate each mystery of her Son's life, she invites us to do as she did at the Annunciation: to ask humbly the questions which open us to the light, in order to end with the obedience of faith" (14).

I once had the great privilege of being a concelebrant at a Mass with Pope John Paul II at Castel Gandolfo near Rome. Once Mass was over, the pope greeted personally each member of the small group of people present. At such times it was the Holy Father's custom to give each visitor a rosary.

One young mother approached the pope holding her young daughter in her arms. After the Holy Father spoke a few words to the woman and gave her a rosary, the young mother turned to go. But the pope thought again and stopped the woman. Taking a second rosary, Pope John Paul pressed it into the tiny hand of the toddler in her mother's arms. The Vicar of Christ wanted to be sure that that little girl had what we all need: her own "doorway to the depths of the Heart of Christ." It is ours through Our Lady of the Rosary.

ch a p t e r   f o u r t e e n

OUR LADY OF GUADALUPE
The Arrival of the Sign of New Life

THE BOOK OF REVELATION DESCRIBES A GLORIOUS
vision: "A great sign appeared in the sky, a woman clothed with
the sun, with the moon under her feet" (Revelation 12:1). What
if this vision were to come true?

In fact, that is exactly what happened in Mexico between
December 9 and December 12, 1531, barely ten years after the
Spanish Captain Hernando Cortés conquered the Aztec Empire.
The Blessed Virgin Mary appeared in this manner to a humble
fifty-seven-year-old widowed peasant named Juan Diego. And
thanks to his dutiful obedience to the one he addressed as "Little
Patroness, Lady, Queen, my Daughter, the Youngest one, my
Little Girl, my Little Virgin, Child, my Mistress,"[1] we continue
to behold the miraculous image of Our Lady of Guadalupe per-
manently emblazoned on Juan Diego's *tilma*—his cloak.

There is no natural explanation why, almost five hundred years
later, the image "inscribed" on St. Juan Diego's *tilma* still exists.

And yet it does, which means that God must have a reason for wanting us to see it.

In 1752 the archbishop of Mexico, Manuel Rubio y Salinas, sent Jesuit Fr. Juan Francisco Lopez to Rome as his envoy. Fr. Lopez's mission was to secure the Holy See's official approval of the Guadalupe apparition and to petition the Holy Father, Pope Benedict XIV, to sanction a special Divine Office and a Mass in honor of Our Lady of Guadalupe.

As Fr. Lopez stood stating his case before the pontiff, he unrolled a canvas bearing a painted reproduction of Mary's miraculous portrait. According to eyewitnesses, when Pope Benedict saw the beautiful figure of Our Lady of Guadalupe, he fell to his knees before it in veneration, weeping. It moved him to exclaim (quoting Psalm 147:20), *Non fecit taliter omni nationi*, "God has not done this for other nations."

The twentieth-century Catholic philosopher Louis Lavelle wrote that "good must be shown to us in order that we may be able to yield to the inclination that bears us toward it."[2] This is what happened to Pope Benedict XIV when he beheld the "good" of Our Lady of Guadalupe; he afterward quickly granted Fr. Lopez's requests. What moved the Holy Father was not simply the exquisite artistic beauty of the now famous image; even more it was the beauty of the *relationship* that the figure represents, the beauty of the *encounter* that Our Lady of Guadalupe offers everyone who gazes upon her image.

As Fr. Joseph Vidal de Figueroa explained in a sermon about Our Lady of Guadalupe in 1660:

> God made use of the means of the painting of this
> image because that which is the most admirable of his

wisdom is how flexible the efficacy of his grace is, always conforming itself to the nature of the one whom it bends. There is no means more efficacious for making an unlettered person understand a great deal once and for all, as to place a picture before such a person.[3]

The Place to Which Mary Came

Our Lady was sent to a people sorely in need of the mercy she modeled. The Aztecs of Mexico worshiped the natural forces upon which they relied—the sun, rain, wind, fire, and plants such as corn and maguey—personifying them as gods and goddesses. Idols of these deities were fashioned and erected in the pyramid temples. Responding to their felt need to appease these deities, and in order to stave off disasters such as famine, earthquake, and disease, the Aztecs made continuous sacrifices—human sacrifices. These "people of the sun" feared that, without the constant offering of sacrificed human hearts to the sun god, he might fail one day to rise in the east.

On some days the victims numbered in the thousands. The hearts of the still alive victims were torn out of their bodies by chanting priests. The Aztecs believed that each victim was a "star" that would reinforce with his sacrificed life the life of the sun god, nourishing him with magical sustenance. Through this collaboration with the gods, the Aztecs supposed they played their part in maintaining the cosmic order of a world threatened by the powers of darkness.

Into this mentality came the glorious Mother of God.

The Guadalupe apparitions took place on the summit of a small hill named Tepeyac, where once had stood a temple to the great mother god Tonantizin, whose head and garments were a mass of writing snakes. At the time of the apparitions, the Spanish Franciscan missionaries, who arrived in Mexico shortly after the Spanish conquerors, were preparing their converts for the Feast of the Immaculate Conception, whom they referred to in their sermons as "she who crushes the serpent." The Guadalupe event demonstrates how the Blessed Virgin Mary elects to come to us in the places where we are most preoccupied by idols of our own making, so that by her presence they will be undone.

The "first impression" of Our Lady of Guadalupe on the indigenous people must have been shocking. The etymology of the name *Mexico* is "Mex (tli)-Xic (tli)-Co"—moon-center-in, or "in the center of the moon." For the Aztecs the moon signified a principal deity, the feathered serpent-god Quetzalcoatl. As the people, habitually accustomed to reading pictographs, looked at the image of the Guadalupana, they would judge that Mary had clearly vanquished Quetzalcoatl, for she stood with her foot planted on a crescent moon.

Similarly, by virtue of the fact that the Lady stood in front of the sun, the Aztecs realized that this Woman was greater than the dreaded sun-god Huitzilopochtli. Fr. Joseph Vidal de Figueroa remarked on this aspect of the miraculous apparition in a sermon: "Mary appears in Mexico without the child God in her arms but rather surrounded by light, because the most stupendous thing about the miracle is how ancient the mystery is, since it brings its origin from all eternity, when the Son of God was light: *erat lux vera* (John 1:9)."[4]

A later Guadalupan sermon, by Fr. Luis de Santa Theresa in 1682, draws attention to the role of light:

> Let it be said that when Mary, the Divine Aurora, appeared in her Conception, peace was made between

God and sinners, between the night and the day, by her shining forth like a light between two lights, human and divine.... Mary was (says St. Peter Damian)...the end of the past night and the beginning of the following day. She was the Aurora who put an end to the shadows of sin and began the lights of grace.[5]

This theme continues into the eighteenth century with Fr. Antonio Lopez Murto's 1792 homily: "The Guadalupana is that bright Sun from whose heat and radiance no inhabitant of America can hide."[6]

In addition, the blue-green hue of Mary's mantle was a color reserved exclusively for Aztec royalty; hence the Lady was a queen. Moreover, the stars, which seemed to have been plucked from heaven and transplanted to Our Lady's mantle, conveyed to the Aztecs that this woman was greater than the stars above, which they worshiped as gods. Particularly striking was the black cross adorning the Lady's gold brooch, for this was the cross that graced the banners and helmets of the Spanish conquerors. This Lady belonged to their religion.

"Am I Not Here Who Am Your Mother?"

In the early morning of what was then the Feast of the Immaculate Conception (December 9, 1531), a recent convert to Christianity named Juan Diego, from the village of Cuautitlan, set out on the long walk to Tlaltelolco to attend Mass. As he drew close to Tepeyac Hill, Juan Diego heard a woman calling him by his Christian name (not his Cuautlitlan name, Cuauhtlatoatzin) and even using the affectionate ending *tzin:* "Juantzin Juan Diegotzin!" The respect and tenderness that Juan Diego experienced in that loving call moved him to follow the voice and climb the 130-foot hill.

There a young lady of utterly sublime brilliance and beauty (she appeared to be as young as fourteen) beckoned and addressed him. Of all the words that Our Lady spoke to Juan Diego, these especially move us to our depths:

> Know for certain that I am the perfect and ever Virgin Mary, Mother of the True God for whom we live.... Here I will show and offer all my love, my compassion, my help, and protection to the people. I am your merciful Mother, the Mother of all who love me, of those who cry to me, of those who have confidence in me. Here I will hear their weeping and their sorrows,... their necessities and misfortunes.... Listen and let it penetrate your heart.... Do not be troubled or weighed down with grief. Do not fear any illness or vexation, anguish or pain. Am I not here who am your Mother? Are you not under my shadow and protection? Am I not your fountain of life? Are you not in the folds of my mantle? In the crossing of my arms? Is there anything else you need? Do not grieve or be disturbed by anything.[7]

Our Lady's message promises three things:

- First, Mary is the Mother of God and our Mother; recognizing this gives us *certainty*. Certainty is something that enters our life and bonds us to it. Certainty is Someone who has happened to us.
- Second, by the power of her maternal presence, the Blessed Mother anticipates all of our suffering and need and effectively provides for them.

- Third, knowledge of Our Lady's closeness and solicitude endows us with the ability to live without fear, grief, or disturbance.

Sacramented Here on Earth

Our Lady revealed to Juan Diego that she wished that a temple be erected at the place of the apparition. The Blessed Virgin then commissioned Juan Diego to relate her "great desire" to the local bishop, Bishop Zumarraga. Receptive but unconvinced, the bishop instructed Juan Diego to return to him with a sign from heaven.

Juan Diego went off to his beloved Lady to communicate the bishop's request. The Blessed Mother promised to provide the sought-after sign.

In the meantime Juan Diego's uncle, Juan Bernardino (who had raised Juan Diego after the early death of the boy's parents), was deathly ill with fever. The dying man begged his nephew to bring him a priest. Thus, on the morning of December 12, instead of going to Tepeyac Hill for his rendezvous with the Blessed Virgin, Juan Diego deliberately evaded the place of the apparition so as to avoid meeting the Lady. But Our Lady of Guadalupe anticipated her servant's detour and met him on his wayward path. Again, it is in just such places that Our Lady takes the initiative to come to us with her maternal presence, speaking words of consolation and hope.

Promising to tend to the dying uncle herself (which she did!), the Blessed Virgin sent Juan Diego to the top of Tepeyac, where, in the spot where Mary once stood, now a miraculous crop of flowers waited to be picked. The climate was too cold and the terrain too contrary ever to produce such magnificent blooms, including Castilian roses. Juan Diego cut the roses and put them in his *tilma*. He returned to Our Lady, and she arranged the gathered flowers in the cloak.

Then Juan Diego proceeded back to the bishop's palace and, when finally granted an audience, let fall his *tilma*. Over the heap of impossible flowers on the floor glowed the glorious image of Our Lady of Guadalupe on Juan Diego's cloak.

What struck most those who saw the sight? Perhaps it was the angel below the Virgin's feet, whose presence signals the heavenly source of the image. Perhaps it was the black cincture around the waist of the Lady, indicating that the Woman is with child (the Spanish expression for "pregnant" is *encinta*, or literally, "adorned with ribbon").

Perhaps it was that the Lady seems to hold one of the nine heart-shaped flowers on her tunic between her hands in a gesture of prayer and offering to God. The Totonac people of San Miguel de Zozocolco, Veracruz, have a prayer to Our Lady of Guadalupe: "Our elders offered hearts to the gods so that there would be harmony in their lives. This Woman says that, without tearing them out, we should place our own hearts in her hands so that she may present them to the true God."[8]

Perhaps it was the inimitable expression on the Lady's face; the fact that she is looking down, in a gesture of respect, signifies that there is someone even greater than she who sends her. Her humble, tender, loving gaze shows her to be a mother contemplating her child.

Perhaps it was that the figure of Our Lady seems to increase in size as one draws back from the image, or perhaps it was the mysterious changing colors observable in the image. Or perhaps it was that, with the figure's knee clearly bent in movement beneath her dress, the Lady appears to be dancing.

What they could not see at the time is that Our Lady of Guadalupe intended us to see *what she was seeing* on that grace-filled day. Scientific research on the *tilma* reveals that microscopic images of Juan Diego, Bishop Zumarraga, and others are reflected in both eyes of Our Lady. This suggests that she was an invisible presence in the room when Juan Diego presented the flowers; Mary chose to include a picture of herself *as she stood watching the scene.* The fact that these figures actually inhabit the eyes of the Blessed Mother gives new meaning to Christ's command, "Behold, your son."

Fr. Francisco de Fuentes y Carrion, in a sermon preached in 1707, sums up the mystery of Our Lady of Guadalupe: "Mary's coming down from heaven and remaining (in a certain sense) Sacramented her on the earth and hidden among humanity until the end of the world. And why? I will tell you why: in order not to leave us alone here on earth."[9]

The Graces of Guadalupe

The miracles associated with the Guadalupe event are countless. Chief among them is the fact that Juan Diego's *tilma* even exists. The cloak is made of frail ayate fibers, which typically disintegrate after twenty years.

Add to that the corrosive smoke of countless votive candles along with the myriad venerating hands that came in contact with the cloak over the decades. For 116 years the sacred image was exposed without any kind of protection; it was placed in a glass case only in 1647. The most celebrated Mexican painter of the later eighteenth century, Miguel Cabrera (who was commissioned to paint the reproduction of the sacred image presented to

Pope Benedict XIV), recorded that on one occasion he saw the *tilma* touched with various objects five hundred times in the space of two hours.[10]

What is more, the *tilma* has proven to be indestructible. An accidental spill of nitric acid over the left side of the image in 1785 left the fabric undamaged. And a 1921 bomb placed at the feet of the image bent the heavy iron crucifix on the altar and blew out the windows of the neighbors but did no harm whatsoever to the image or to the glass shielding it.

These marvels move us to join in the wonder expressed by Fr. Francisco Xavier Rodriguez in his 1766 sermon: "To what end did Mary arrange to remain among us in such a wonderful way, leaving us in this Linen a species of sacrament of her Love toward us?"[11] An exact copy of the sacred image was placed in the cabin of Admiral Andrea Doria, who led the victorious—and decisive—Battle of Lepanto in 1571.

But more awesome than anything else is the fact that, as a direct result of the Guadalupe apparitions, the greatest mass conversion to Christianity in all of history happened: Over nine million Aztecs converted. Contemplating this mystery, the Dominican preacher Juan de Villa y Sanchez says in a 1733 sermon: "The three Magi were guided to the manger of the recently born God by a star.... America had to find Christ with a better Star than that with which Asia, Africa, and Europe found him; because the star of those three kings was a material star, which appeared in heaven; the Star of America had to be, as was the great Lady, one which appeared on earth."[12]

In the Veracruz region of Mexico, before a priest celebrates Mass on the Feast of Our Lady of Guadalupe, the people tell him:

Focus on the womb of this woman, who dances with the joy of the feast, because she will give us her Son. With the harmony of the angel holding heaven and earth [referring to her mantle and gown], a new life is extended. This is what we received from our elders: that our own life does not end, but has a new meaning, and as the Great Book of the Spaniards [the Bible; see Revelation 12:1] says: There was a sign in heaven, a woman dressed with the sun, with the moon under her feet and a crown of stars, and she is about to give birth. This is what we are celebrating, Father: the arrival of this sign of unity, harmony, and new life.[13]

When we live the mystery of Our Lady of Guadalupe, we want to join in the ancient Mexican song that was adapted in honor of the transition of the sacred image from the cathedral to its new home in Tepeyac on December 23, 1531:

I have heard Holy Mary singing:
"I am the precious plant with hidden buds."
...Delicately was your image painted,
And on the sacred canvas, your soul was concealed.
All is perfect and complete in its presence,
And there, God willing, I shall dwell for ever.[14]

chapter fifteen

THE SATURDAY MEMORIAL OF THE
BLESSED VIRGIN MARY
Embracing Mary's Memory

THE DIRECTORY ON POPULAR PIETY AND THE LITURGY,
published by the Vatican Congregation for Divine Worship,
states:

> Saturdays stand out among those days dedicated to the
> Virgin Mary. These are designated as *memorials of the
> Blessed Virgin Mary....*
>
> ...[T]oday the memorial rightly emphasizes certain
> values "to which contemporary spirituality is more sen-
> sitive: it is a remembrance of the maternal example and
> discipleship of the Blessed Virgin Mary who, strength-
> ened by faith and hope, on that great Saturday on which
> Our Lord lay in the tomb, was the only one of the dis-
> ciples to hold vigil in expectation of the Lord's resurrec-
> tion; it is prelude and introduction to the celebration of

Sunday, the weekly memorial of the resurrection of Christ; it is a sign that the "Virgin Mary is continuously present and operative in the life of the Church." [1]

Joining in Mary's Interior Conversation

The Church's gift of the Saturday memorial of the Blessed Virgin Mary is a means by which we can reverently remember Mary *and* participate in the way that Mary remembers. Pope Benedict XVI provides a beautiful little catechesis on "memory" and "memorial" in his book *Jesus of Nazareth*. He writes: "Mary's memory is first of all a retention of…events in remembrance, but it is more than that: It is an interior conversation with all that has happened. Thanks to this conversation, she penetrates into the interior dimension, she sees the events in their interconnectedness, and she learns to understand them."[2] The pope insists that being Christian is a result of "an encounter *with an event.*"[3]

An event is something that gets our attention, engaging and moving us. It is a happening that never loses its newness, its freshness—a happening that, in a certain respect, *keeps* happening: It enhances, shapes, and energizes our life. An event has an indelible effect on us, awakening us and making us alert, animating us. There's something irresistible and compelling about an event that makes it stand out from mere occurrences.

The lasting influence of an event informs the way we look at everything around us; our way of judging reality is based on the significant events that have formed (and continue to transform) our life. An event from earlier in our life changes—even determines—our here and now. The reason why a married couple celebrate their wedding anniversary every year is because it is an event that impacts and implicates every dimension of the moment-by-moment life they live together.

Thus, when it comes to our faith, we want to see the event of Jesus Christ in the way that the Blessed Virgin Mary did. We want to penetrate to the interior dimension of the Christ event and understand it with the disposition of the Mother of God. The celebration of the Marian Saturday memorial is a way to enter into an interior conversation with the life, death, and resurrection of Jesus Christ, united personally with the Blessed Virgin Mary. By observing the memorial of Mary, we experience "the memory of Christ": the consciousness of his presence in us and in the concrete circumstances of our life.

Memory, Mary, and the Holy Spirit

Memory moves us to return to the truest source of our life—to what fills our life with meaning and fulfillment. The more we reflect on something, the more we grasp it and become one with it. Through memory, says Pope Benedict XVI, an event "becomes intelligible at a level beyond the merely factual. Memory sheds light on the sense of the act, which then acquires a deeper meaning.... 'Remembrance'...makes it possible to enter into the interiority of the events, into the intrinsic coherence of God's speaking and acting."[4] That is, thanks to memory, we do not regard things at the level of mere appearances, but we gain access to the "inside" of things—to their essence.

Put more simply, in the Saturday memorial of the Blessed Virgin Mary, we are in effect saying:

> Loving Mother, we want what happened to us when Christ first called us and claimed us to happen again. We want to cherish that encounter. But we do not want to rely on our thoughts, our ideas, our feelings, or our preconceptions of the events that saved us; we want to

experience anew the event of Christ united with your heart, your mind, and your soul, for no one can know and love and serve Jesus Christ as you do. Let us live your memory of Jesus, so that we can enter into the event of Christ's love, see the truest meaning of all his actions, and live his love with your awareness of its meaning.

After the Ascension Mary was present in the upper room with the apostles as they devoted themselves to prayer (see Acts 1:14). She served as a "memory" for the nascent Church. By her presence the followers of Christ could better see the interconnectedness of the wondrous events that had just transpired. The Mother of God's presence shed light on the deepest meaning of Christ's resurrection and ascension. Because Mary was with them, the disciples could more effectively enter into the events of salvation they had witnessed, so as to grasp their intrinsic coherence. Things made more sense in her. God would always speak to them—and to us—through those events, and the presence of Mary attuned them to hear God's voice.

Pope Benedict says, "The Church's remembering…transcends the sphere of our own human understanding and knowing. It is a being-led by the Holy Spirit, who shows us the connectedness of Scripture, the connection between word and reality, and, in doing that, leads us 'into all the truth.'"[5] No wonder the Church is eager weekly to celebrate the memorial of the Virgin who was herself espoused by the Holy Spirit.

"[B]y remembering," says Pope Benedict XVI, "the believer enters into the depth of the event and sees what could not be seen on an immediate and merely superficial level. But in so doing he does not move away from the reality; rather, he comes to know it more deeply and thus sees the truth concealed in the outward act."[6]

We welcome the Saturday memorial of the Blessed Virgin Mary as a way of coming to know reality more deeply and of seeing the truth concealed in every gesture of our Savior. Thus with Mary we can say yes to that truth.

notes

PREFACE

1. Thérèse of Lisieux, *Her Last Conversations*, trans. John Clarke (Washington, D.C.: ICS, 1977), pp. 161–162.
2. Thomas Aquinas, *Summa Theologiae*, vol. 3, trans. Samuel Parsons and Albert Pinheiro (Cambridge, Mass.: Cambridge University Press, 1971), IIIa, 45. 3.

CHAPTER ONE. WHY PRAY TO MARY?: SEVEN REASONS FOR MARIAN DEVOTION

1. John Paul II, writing sometime before or around March 1, 1997.
2. Louis-Marie de Montfort, *True Devotion to the Blessed Virgin*, trans. Malachy Gerard Carroll (Boston: Daughters of Saint Paul, 1982), p. 184.
3. De Montfort, *True Devotion*, p. 77.
4. De Montfort, *True Devotion*, p. 25.
5. James Walsh, trans., *Julian of Norwich: Showings* (New York: Paulist, 1978), pp. 222–223.
6. Peter Chrysologus, quoted in Luigi Gambero, *Mary and the Fathers of the Church: The Blessed Virgin Mary in Patristic Thought*, trans. Thomas Buffer (San Francisco: Ignatius, 1999), p. 300.
7. Methodius, quoted in David Supple, ed., *Virgin Wholly Marvelous: Praises of Our Lady by the Popes, Councils, Saints, and Doctors of the Church* (Cambridge, Mass.: Ravengate, 1981), p. 114.
8. Bernard of Clairvaux, quoted in Luigi Gambero, *Mary in the Middle Ages: The Blessed Virgin Mary in the Thought of the Medieval Latin Theologians*, trans. Thomas Buffer (San Francisco: Ignatius, 2005), p. 136.
9. De Montfort, *True Devotion*, p. 52.
10. Ildephonsus, quoted in Supple, p. 59.
11. Anselm of Canterbury, quoted in Gambero, *Mary in the Middle Ages*, p. 113.
12. John Berchmans, quoted in Supple, p. 113.

13. Origen, *Commentary on John* 1:6, quoted in Gambero, *Mary and the Fathers of the Church*, p. 80.

14. Walsh, *Julian of Norwich: Showings*, p. 222.

15. De Montfort, *True Devotion*, p. 52.

16. John of Avila, quoted in Supple, p. 25.

17. John of Damascus, quoted in de Montfort, *True Devotion*, p. 25.

18. Suzanne Noffke, trans., *Catherine of Siena: The Dialogue* (New York: Paulist, 1980), p. 286.

19. De Montfort, *True Devotion*, p. 59.

20. De Montfort, *True Devotion*, pp. 25–26.

21. De Montfort, *True Devotion*, p. 120.

22. De Montfort, *True Devotion*, p. 126.

23. Amadeus of Lausanne, quoted in Supple, p. 25.

24. Ildephonsus, quoted in Supple, p. 156

25. Germanus of Constantinople, quoted in Supple, p. 156.

26. Peter Damian, quoted in Supple, p. 157.

27. Bernard of Clairvaux, cited in De Montfort, *True Devotion*, p. 102.

28. Thomas Aquinas, quoted in Supple, p. 158.

29. Bridget of Sweden, quoted in Alphonsus Liguori, *The Glories of Mary*, ed. Dennis Billy and Charles G. Fehrenbach (Liguori, Mo.: Liguori, 2000), p. 339.

30. Antoninus, quoted in Supple, p. 160.

31. Lawrence of Brindisi, quoted in Supple, p. 164.

32. John Eudes, quoted in Supple, p. 161.

33. Alphonsus Liguori, quoted in Supple, p. 161.

34. De Montfort, *True Devotion*, p. 10.

35. De Montfort, *True Devotion*, p. 14.

36. John of Avila, quoted in Supple, p. 24.

37. Aelred of Rievaulx, quoted in Gambero, *Mary and the Fathers of the Church*, p. 165.

38. De Montfort, *True Devotion*, p. 20.

39. De Montfort, *True Devotion*, p. 88.

40. De Montfort, *True Devotion*, p. 114.

41. De Montfort, *True Devotion*, p. 41.

42. De Montfort, *True Devotion*, p. 115.

43. De Montfort, *True Devotion*, p. 6.

44. De Montfort, *True Devotion*, p. 119.

45. Jacques Benigne Bossuet, *Devotion to the Blessed Virgin: Being the Substance of All the Sermons for Mary's Feasts Throughout the Year*, trans. F.M. Capes (London: Longmans, Green, 1899), p. 71.

46. Alain de Lille, quoted in Gambero, *Mary in the Middle Ages*, p. 187.

47. De Montfort, *True Devotion*, p. 30.

48. John Paul II, *Theotokos: Woman, Mother, Disciple: A Catechesis on Mary, Mother of God* (Boston: Pauline, 2000), pp. 192, 219.

49. De Montfort, *True Devotion*, p. 190.

50. Jerome, quoted in Supple, p. 114.

51. Antonio Lopez Murto, quoted in Francisco Raymond Schulte, *Mexican Spirituality: Its Sources and Mission in the Earliest Guadalupan Sermons* (Lanham, Md.: Rowman & Littlefield, 2002), pp. 58–59.

52. Bonaventure, quoted in Supple, p. 130.

53. De Montfort, *True Devotion*, p. 162.

CHAPTER TWO. THE IMMACULATE CONCEPTION: HOW GOD CONCEIVES OF HIS OWN GOODNESS

1. Joseph Ratzinger, *Daughter Zion: Meditations on the Church's Marian Belief*, trans. John M. McDermott (San Francisco: Ignatius, 1983), pp. 70–71.

2. Thomas Aquinas, quoted in Supple, p. 19.

3. John Paul II, *Theotokos*, p. 43.

4. Anselm, quoted in *The Liturgy of the Hours* (New York: Catholic Book, 1975), vol. 1, p. 1228.

5. Bede the Venerable, quoted in Gambero, *Mary in the Middle Ages*, p. 37.

6. John Paul II, *Theotokos*, p. 63.

7. Anselm, quoted in *Liturgy of the Hours*, vol. 1, p. 1228.

8. Ambrose Autpert, *De Assumptione sanctae Mariae* 4, quoted in Gambero, *Mary in the Middle Ages*, pp. 49–50.

9. John of Damascus, quoted in Supple, p. 47.

10. John Henry Newman, *The Mystical Rose: Thoughts on the Blessed Virgin from the Writings of John Henry Cardinal Newman* (New York: Scepter, 1996), p. 92.

11. Anselm, quoted in *Liturgy of the Hours*, vol. 1, pp. 1228, 1229.

12. John Paul II, *Theotokos*, p. 42.

13. Anselm, quoted in *Liturgy of the Hours*, vol. 1, p. 1229, emphasis added.

14. Jonathan Yardley, "Beyond the Fringes," *Smithsonian*, September 2007, Volume 38, Number 6, p. 24.

15. De Montfort, *True Devotion*, p. 14.

16. Anselm, quoted in *Liturgy of the Hours*, vol. 1, p. 1229.

17. Louis Lavelle, *The Dilemma of Narcissus* (Burdett, N.Y.: Larson, 1993), pp. 217, 215.

18. Benedict XVI, *Deus Caritas Est*, Encyclical on Christian Love, no. 1, December 25, 2005, www.vatican.va.

19. De Montfort, *True Devotion*, p. 120.

20. John Paul II, *Theotokos*, p. 44.

CHAPTER THREE. THE BIRTH OF MARY: THE BIRTH OF THE MOTHER OF OUR REBIRTH

1. Romanos, *Hymn 2 on Christmas*, quoted in Gambero, *Mary and the Fathers of the Church*, p. 327.

2. See Hugo Rahner, *Our Lady and the Church*, trans. Sebastian Bullough (Bethesda, Md.: Zaccaheus, 2004), pp. 30-31.

3. John Tauler, *Spiritual Conferences* (Charlotte, N.C.: TAN, 1978), pp. 168–169, 171.

4. Joseph Raya and José de Vinck, *Byzantine Daily Worship: With Byzantine Breviary, the Three Liturgies, Propers of the Day and Various Offices* (Allendale, N.J.: Alleluia, 1969), p. 439.

5. Gregory Palamas, *The Saving Work of Christ: Sermons by Saint Gregory Palamas*, ed. Christopher Veniamin (South Canaan, Pa.: Mount Thabor, 2008), p. 4.

6. Andrew of Crete, from *The Liturgy of the Hours*, Birthday of Mary, September 8, quoted at www.crossroadsinitiative.com.

7. Adapted from Jean Baptiste Marie Vianney, *Sermons for the Sundays and Feasts of the Year* (Long Prairie, Minn.: Neumann, 1901), p. 252.

8. John Damascene, quoted in Supple, p. 5.

9. Gregory Palamas, p. 2.

10. Bossuet, pp. 40–41.

11. Gregory Palamas, p. 2.

12. Paul the Deacon, Homily 45, *In Assumptione*, quoted in Gambero, *Mary in the Middle Ages*, p. 58.

13. Bridget of Sweden, *Sermo angelicus*, book 3, quoted in Gambero, *Mary in the Middle Ages*, p. 277.

14. Marian Prayer of Catherine of Siena, in Virgilio Noe, ed., *Prayers to Mary* (New York: Catholic Book, 1987), p. 54.

15. Rainer Maria Rilke, "The Birth of the Virgin Mary," *The Life of the Virgin Mary: A Cycle of Poems*, trans. Christine McNeill (Dublin: Dedalus, 2003), p. 9.

16. Andrew of Crete, from *Liturgy of the Hours*, www.crossroadsinitiative.com.

17. Louis de Montfort, "Love of Eternal Wisdom," in *God Alone: The Collected Writings of St. Louis Marie de Montfort* (Bay Shore, N.Y.: Montfort, 1995), pp. 78–79.

18. Henry Suso, *Wisdom's Watch Upon the Hours*, vol. 4, *The Fathers of the Church*, trans. Edmund Colledge (Washington, D.C.: Catholic University of America Press, 1994), p. 222.

19. Gregory Palamas, p. 3.

20. Marian Prayer of St. Catherine of Siena, in Noe, pp. 52–54.

CHAPTER FOUR. THE PRESENTATION OF MARY: SELF-DONATION AS DESTINY

1. Bridget of Sweden, *Revelations of St. Bridget, on the Life and Passion of Our Lord and the Life of His Blessed Mother* (Charlotte, N.C.: TAN, 1984), pp. 18–19.

2. Julian Carron, quoted in *The Destiny of Man: Exercises of the Fraternity of Communion and Liberation* (Rimini, Italy: Fraternity of Communion and Liberation, 2004), pp. 11, 16.

3. Germanus of Constantinople, quoted in Gambero, *Mary and the Fathers of the Church*, pp. 382–383.

4. *Byzantine Daily Worship*, pp. 516–517.

5. John Paul II, *Rosarium Virginis,* Apostolic Letter on the Most Holy Rosary, October 16, 2002, no. 20, www.vatican.va.

6. Pope John Paul II, *Vita Consecrata*, Apostolic Exhortation on the Consecrated Life, March 25, 1996, nos. 20, 16, www.vatican.va.

7. Rilke, "The Presentation of the Virgin Mary in the Temple," pp. 10–11.

8. *Collection of Masses of the Blessed Virgin Mary, Volume 1: Sacramentary* (New York: Catholic Book, 1992), p. 203.

9. *Byzantine Daily Worship*, pp. 516–517.

10. John Eudes, *Meditations on Various Subjects,* trans. Charles Lebrun (New Providence, N.Y.: P.J. Kenedy, 1947), p. 215.

11. Sor Juana Inés de la Cruz, "Poem II for the Feast of the Presentation of Our Lady," in Pamela Kirk Rappaport, trans., *Sor Juana Inés de la Cruz: Selected Writings* (Mahwah, N.J.: Paulist, 2005), pp. 45–46.

CHAPTER FIVE. THE ANNUNCIATION: THE YES THAT MAKES THE IMPOSSIBLE POSSIBLE

1. Bossuet, p. 69.

2. Rilke, "The Annunciation," p. 12.

3. Romanos, *On the Annunciation* 1, 1, quoted in Gambero, *Mary and the Fathers of the Church*, p. 329.

4. *Byzantine Daily Worship*, p. 661.

5. Bossuet, p. 2.

6. Ambrose, quoted in Gambero, *Mary and the Fathers of the Church*, p. 201.

7. Thérèse of Lisieux, http://legion-of-mary-ny.home.att.net.

8. Catherine of Siena, *The Prayers of Catherine of Siena,* 2nd ed. (San Jose, Calif.: Authors Choice, 2001), p. 188.

9. Lavelle, *Dilemma*, pp. 146–147.

10. Luigi Giussani, quoted in introduction to the CD *Divina Liturgia di san Giovanni Crisostomo*, op. 31, no. 21, trans. Susan Scott (Milan: Fraternita di Comunione e Liberazione, Cooperativa Editoriale

Nuovo Mondo), p. 16.

11. Raniero Cantalamessa, *Life in Christ: A Spiritual Commentary on the Letter to the Romans*, trans. Frances Lonergan Villa (Collegeville, Minn.: Liturgical, 1994), p. 172.

12. Joseph Ratzinger, *Dogma and Preaching*, trans. Matthew J. O'Connell (Chicago: Franciscan Herald, 1985), pp. 78–79.

13. Bossuet, p. 71.

14. Bossuet, pp. 72–73.

15. Robert Southwell, "Our Ladie's Salutation," *The Complete Poems of Robert Southwell, S.J.*, ed. Alexander B. Grosart (New York: AMS, 1971), p. 121.

16. Luigi Giussani, *You Live for Love of Something Happening Now: Exercises of the Fraternity of Communion and Liberation* (Rimini, Italy: Fraternity of Communion and Liberation, 2006), p. 20.

17. Southwell, p. 121.

18. See de Montfort, *True Devotion*, p. 184.

19. John Paul II, *Redemptoris Mater*, Encyclical Letter on the Blessed Virgin Mary in the Life of the Pilgrim Church, March 25, 1987 (Vatican: Libreria Editrice Vaticana, 1987), no. 33.

20. De Montfort, *True Devotion*, p. 182.

21. Guerric of Igny, *Liturgical Sermons: Volume Two—Cistercian Fathers Series: Number Thirty-Two* (Spencer, Mass.: Cistercian, 1971), pp. 32, 33, 34.

22. Thomas of Villanova, quoted in Supple, p. 30.

23. Leo the Great, quoted in Rahner, p. 33.

24. John Paul II, *Redemptoris Mater*, no. 28, quoting *Roman Missal*, formula of the consecration of the wine in the Eucharistic Prayers.

25. See Jacobus de Voragine, *The Golden Legend: Readings on the Saints*, trans. William Granger Ryan (Princeton, N.J.: Princeton University Press, 1993), p. 199.

26. Joseph Ratzinger, *Introduction to Christianity*, trans. J.R. Foster (San Francisco: Ignatius, 2004), p. 211.

27. Julian Carron, quoted in *You Live for Love*, pp. 33, 34.

28. Jacob of Serug, "Homily 1," in *On the Mother of God*, trans. Mary Hansbury (Crestwood, N.Y.: St. Vladimir's Seminary Press, 1998), p. 29.

29. Gabriel Marcel, quoted in Ralph Harper, *On Presence: Variations and Reflections* (Baltimore: Johns Hopkins University Press, 1991), p. 43.

30. *Traces*, June 10, 2004, pp. 28–30.

31. Thomas Aquinas, cited in Bossuet, p. 3.

32. De Montfort, *True Devotion*, p. 12.

33. Bossuet, p. 3.

34. Guerric of Igny, quoted in *Christ Our Light, Patristic Readings on Gospel Themes*, ed. Friends of Henry Ashworth (Riverdale, Md.: Exordium, 1981), vol. 1, p. 64.

35. Rupert of Deutz, quoted in Gambero, *Mary in the Middle Ages*, p. 126.

36. De Montfort, *True Devotion*, p. 10.

37. Rahner, p. 76.

38. De Montfort, *True Devotion*, pp. 21–22, 12.

39. Ildephonsus, "Holy Virgin, I Beg You," in Noe, pp. 36, 37.

40. Ambrose, quoted in Supple, p. 53.

CHAPTER SIX. THE VISITATION: HOW THE CLOSENESS OF JESUS COMES TO US

1. Bonaventure, Sermon 4 of the Annunciation, quoted in Gambero, *Mary in the Middle Ages*, p. 209.

2. Joseph Ratzinger, *The Feast of Faith: Approaches to a Theology of the Liturgy*, trans. Graham Harrison (San Francisco: Ignatius, 1986), pp. 150–151.

3. Gabriel Marcel, quoted in Harper, p. 42.

4. Harper, p. 44.

5. Lavelle, *Dilemma*, pp. 164–165.

6. Rilke, "The Visitation," p. 13.

7. Bossuet, pp. 89–90.

8. John Paul II, *Rosarium Virginis Mariae*, no. 11.

9. Harold Holzer, "Election Day 1860," *Smithsonian*, November 2008, p. 92.

10. Caryll Houselander, *The Reed of God* (Allen, Tex.: Christian Classics, 1944), p. 34.
11. Bossuet, p. 92.
12. Athanasius, quoted in Gambero, *Mary and the Fathers of the Church*, p. 105.
13. Ambrose, cited by Bossuet, p. 5.
14. Peter Chrysologus, *St. Peter Chrysologus: Selected Sermons, Volume 2*, vol. 109, *The Fathers of the Church*, trans. William B. Palardy (Washington, D.C.: Catholic University of America Press, 2004), pp. 293–294.
15. Ambrose, quoted in Claire Russell, ed., *Glimpses of the Church Fathers: Selections from the Writings of the Fathers of the Church* (London: Scepter, 1994), pp. 207–208.
16. De Montfort, *True Devotion*, p. 198.
17. Bossuet, p. 88.
18. Francis de Sales, quoted in Supple, p. 160.
19. Bossuet, pp. 83, 84.
20. Jacob of Serug, "Homily III," pp. 78–80, 81.

Chapter Seven. Mary the Mother of God: The Mother We Need for Life

1. John Paul II, *Theotokos*, pp. 59, 215.
2. De Montfort, *True Devotion*, p. 17.
3. Thomas Aquinas, quoted in Supple, p. 63.
4. Bernard of Clairvaux, *In Nativitate* 11, quoted in Gambero, *Mary in the Middle Ages*, p. 133.
5. John Paul II, *Theotokos*, p. 122.
6. Germanus of Constantinople, quoted in Russell, p. 512.
7. Words and music by George Root, http://tripod.com.
8. Teresa of Avila, *The Book of Her Life*, vol. 1, *The Collected Works of St. Teresa of Avila*, trans. Kieran Kavanaugh and Otilio Rodriguez (Washington, D.C.: ICS, 1987), p. 56.
9. Alice Miller, *The Drama of the Gifted Child: The Search for the True Self*, trans. Ruth Ward (New York: Basic, 1997), p. 27.

10. Joseph Ratzinger, *Principles of Catholic Theology*, trans. Mary Frances McCarthy (San Francisco: Ignatius, 1987), pp. 79–80.

11. John Paul II, *Redemptoris Mater*, no. 45

12. Joseph Ratzinger, *In the Beginning...: A Catholic Understanding of the Story of Creation and the Fall*, trans. Boniface Ramsey (Grand Rapids: Eerdmans, 1995), pp. 72–73.

13. Thérèse of Lisieux, *General Correspondence: Volume II*, trans. John Clarke (Washington, D.C.: ICS, 1988), p. 761.

14. John Paul II, *Theotokos*, pp. 150, 152.

15. Hans Urs von Balthasar, *The Grain of Wheat: Aphorisms*, trans. Erasmo Leiva-Merikakis (San Francisco: Ignatius, 1995), pp. 65–66.

16. Nick Beavers, letter to his mother, quoted in Manny Howard, "The Lost Boy," *New York Magazine*, July 24, 1995, p. 35.

17. Germanus of Constantinople, quoted in Russell, p. 512.

18. See Supple, p. 91

19. Noe, p. 10.

20. Von Balthasar, *The Grain of Wheat*, pp. 65, 66.

21. John Paul II, *Gift and Mystery: On the Fiftieth Anniversary of My Priestly Ordination* (New York: Doubleday, 1996), pp. 28–29.

22. Bridget of Sweden, *Revelations*, book 6, quoted in Gambero, *Mary in the Middle Ages*, p. 280.

23. Hans Urs von Balthasar, *The Laity and the Life of the Counsels, The Church's Mission in the World*, trans. Brian McNeil and D.C. Schindler (San Francisco: Ignatius, 2003), pp. 194–195.

24. John Paul II, *Redemptoris Mater*, no. 44.

25. John Paul II, *Theotokos*, p. 42.

26. De Montfort, *True Devotion*, p. 10.

27. Thérèse of Lisieux, *Daily Thoughts From the Little Flower*, trans. Francis Broome (Coopersburg, Pa.: Carmel of the Little Flower, 1964), p. 8.

28. De Montfort, *True Devotion*, pp. 148–149, 150.

29. De Montfort, *True Devotion*, p. 141.

30. De Montfort, *True Devotion*, p. 102.

31. Dionysius the Carthusian, quoted in Gambero, *Mary and the Fathers of the Church*, pp. 310–311.

32. Germanus of Constantinople, quoted in Russell, pp. 511–512.

33. Dante, *The Divine Comedy, The Paradiso*, Canto 33, vv. 1, 16–8, quoted in Noe, pp. 50, 51.

34. De Montfort, *True Devotion*, p. 18.

35. Guerric Igny, quoted in *Christ Our Light*, p. 64.

CHAPTER EIGHT. OUR LADY OF SORROWS: OUR COMPANION IN COMPASSION

1. John Paul II, *Theotokos*, p. 184.

2. Bossuet, pp. 126–127.

3. Alphonsus Liguori, quoted in Supple, p. 74.

4. Bossuet, p. 127.

5. Bonaventure, quoted in Supple, p. 73.

6. Alphonsus Liguori, quoted in Supple, p. 74.

7. Arnold of Bonneval, *De laudibus B.M.V.*, quoted in Gambero, *Mary in the Middle Ages*, p. 150.

8. Anthony of Padua, *Dominica 3 in Quadragesima* 6, quoted in Gambero, *Mary in the Middle Ages*, p. 201.

9. Charles Peguy, *The Mystery of the Charity of Joan of Arc*, trans. Julian Green (New York: Pantheon, 1950), pp. 149–151.

10. John Paul II, *Salvifici Doloris*, Encyclical on the Christian Meaning of Human Suffering, February 11, 1984 (Vatican: Libreria Editrice Vaticana, 1984), no. 2.

11. Benedict XVI, *Spe Salvi*, Encyclical Letter on Christian Hope, November 30, 2007, no. 38, www.vatican.va.

12. Lavelle, *Dilemma*, p. 104.

13. *Faith: The Ultimate Expression of Affection for Oneself* (Milan: Traces Booklets, 2008), p. 8.

14. Ambrose, quoted in Gambero, *Mary and the Fathers of the Church*, p. 203.

15. Alphonsus Liguori, quoted in Supple, p. 91.

16. John Paul II, *Theotokos*, p. 188.

17. John Paul II, *Rosarium Virginis Mariae*, no. 10.

18. Rupert of Deutz, quoted in Gambero, *Mary in the Middle Ages*, p. 130.

19. John Paul II, *Salvifici Doloris*, no. 26.

20. Albert the Great, quoted in Supple, p. 73.

21. Dionysius the Carthusian, quoted in Gambero, *Mary in the Middle Ages*, p. 312.

22. Leo the Great, quoted in Supple, p. 116.

23. Origen, *Commentary on John* 1:6, quoted in Gambero, *Mary and the Fathers of the Church*, p. 80.

24. Melissa Fay Greene, "The Orphan Ranger," *The New Yorker*, July 17, 2000, http://www.melissafaygreene.com.

25. George Bernanos, *The Diary of a Country Priest*, as translated and quoted in John Saward, *The Beauty of Holiness and the Holiness of Beauty: Art, Sanctity, and the Truth of Catholicism* (San Francisco: Ignatius, 1997), pp. 136–137.

26. Amadeus of Lausanne, *Eight Homilies on the Praises of Blessed Mary*, trans. Grace Perigo (Kalamazoo, Mich.: Cistercian, 1979), p. 73.

27. Henry Suso, *Wisdom's Watch Upon the Hours*, vol. 4, *The Fathers of the Church*, trans. Edmund Colledge (Washington, D.C.: Catholic University of America Press, 1994), p. 222.

28. John Paul II, *Redemptor Hominis*, Encyclical Letter The Redeemer of Man (Vatican: Libreria Editrice Vaticana, 1979), no. 45; *Theotokos*, p. 190.

CHAPTER NINE. THE ASSUMPTION: SHARING IN THE MYSTERIES OF HEAVEN

1. Amadeus of Lausanne, *Eight Homilies*, p. 1.

2. John Paul II, *Theotokos*, p. 19.

3. John Paul II, *Theotokos*, p. 36.

4. John Paul II, *Theotokos*, p. 36.

5. John Paul II, *Theotokos*, p. 126.

6. Amadeus of Lausanne, *Eight Homilies*, p. 60.

7. Amadeus of Lausanne, *Eight Homilies*, p. 64.

8. Bossuet, p. 137.

9. Richard Hobbs, *Fifteen Mysteries in the Life of Jesus* (Staten Island, N.Y.: Alba House, 2002), pp. 82–83.

10. Cyril of Alexandria, quoted in Rahner, p. 118.

11. Bridget, *Revelations*, pp. 67–69.

12. Bossuet, p. 138.

13. Francis de Sales, as quoted in John Paul II, *Theotokos*, p. 202.

14. Zbigniew Herbert, *The Collected Poems, 1956–1998*, trans. Alissa Valles (New York: HarperCollins, 2007), p. 440.

15. John of Damascus, quoted in Brian E. Daley, ed., *On the Dormition of Mary: Early Patristic Homilies* (Crestwood, N.Y.: St. Vladimir's Seminary Press, 1998), p. 245.

16. Thomas Aquinas, cited in Supple, p. 103.

17. Germanus of Constantinople, cited in Gambero, *Mary and the Fathers of the Church*, p. 384.

18. John of Damascus, quoted in Daley, pp. 245–246.

19. Rilke, "About the Virgin's Death," p. 27.

20. Bossuet, p. 133.

21. Bernard, quoted in Supple, p. 107.

22. Armenian hymn, quoted in Rahner, p. 132.

23. Sor Juana, "*Villancico* VI for the Feast of the Assumption," p. 50.

24. Bossuet, p. 8.

25. John Paul II, *Theotokos*, p. 31.

26. John Paul II, *Theotokos*, p. 62.

27. John Paul II, *Theotokos*, p. 64.

28. Jean Gerson, *Poetic Works* 164, quoted in Gambero, *Mary in the Middle Ages*, p. 289.

29. Benedict XVI, Homily, Feast of the Assumption, August 15, 2005, www.vatican.va.

30. Andrew of Crete, quoted in Supple, p. 156.

31. Bossuet, p. 90.

32. Germanus of Constantinople, quoted in Gambero, *Mary and the Fathers of the Church*, p. 386.

33. Ronald Knox, *The Pastoral Sermons*, ed. Philip Caraman (Chicago: Franciscan Herald, 1960), pp. 452–453.

34. Amadeus of Lausanne, *Eight Homilies*, p. 14.

35. John Paul II, *Theotokos*, p. 38.

36. John Paul II, *Theotokos*, p. 38.

37. Hildebert of Fontenelle, quoted in Supple, p. 70.

38. Louis of Grenada, *Summa of the Christian Life,* trans. Jordan Aumann (Charlotte, N.C.: TAN, 1979), vol. 3, p. 205.

39. John of Damascus, quoted in Daley, pp. 245–246.

CHAPTER TEN. THE QUEENSHIP OF MARY: INCREASING THE SPLENDOR OF THE ELECT

1. Henry Suso, quoted in Supple, pp. 121–122.

2. Albert the Great, quoted in Supple, p. 71.

3. John Paul II, *Theotokos*, pp. 209–210.

4. Arnold of Bonneval, *De Laudibus B.M.V.*, quoted in Gambero, *Mary in the Middle Ages*, p. 151.

5. Bernardine of Siena, *De salutatione angelica*, sermon 52, quoted in Gambero, *Mary in the Middle Ages*, p. 296.

6. De Montfort, *True Devotion*, p. 1.

7. Anthony of Padua, *In Assumptione* 3, quoted in Gambero, *Mary in the Middle Ages*, p. 200.

8. Thérèse of Lisieux, *Her Last Conversations*, pp. 161–162.

9. John Paul II, *Theotokos*, pp. 211–212.

10. Philip of Harveng, *In Cantica Canticorum* 4, quoted in Gambero, *Mary in the Middle Ages*, p. 184.

11. Thomas Aquinas, quoted in Supple, p. 126.

12. Albert the Great, *De natura boni*, quoted in Gambero, *Mary in the Middle Ages*, p. 229.

13. Paul the Deacon, *Homilia* 45, *In Assumptione*, quoted in Gambero, *Mary in the Middle Ages*, pp. 58–59.

14. Fulbert of Chartres, Sermon 6, quoted in Gambero, *Mary in the Middle Ages*, p. 86.

15. Peter Canisius, quoted in John E. Rotelle, ed., *Day by Day with Mary* (Villanova: Augustinian, 2001), p. 300.

16. De Montfort, *True Devotion*, p. 195.

17. Romanos, *Hymn 2 on Christmas,* 10, quoted in Gambero, *Mary and the Fathers of the Church*, p. 327.

18. G.K. Chesterton, *The Collected Works of G.K. Chesterton* (San Francisco: Ignatius, 1994), vol. 10, pp. 112–114.

19. Eadmer of Canterbury, *De conceptione*, quoted in Gambero, *Mary in the Middle Ages*, p. 123.

20. Peter the Venerable, quoted in Gambero, *Mary in the Middle Ages*, p. 147.

CHAPTER ELEVEN. THE IMMACULATE HEART OF MARY: KNOWING THE MOTHER OF GOD BY HEART

1. De Montfort, *God Alone*, p. 79.

2. John Paul II, *Theotokos*, p. 171.

3. John Eudes, *The Admirable Heart of Mary* (New York: P.J. Kenedy & Sons, 1948), p. 246.

4. Rahner, pp. 104, 107.

5. Augustine, quoted in Rahner, p. 101.

6. Rahner, p. 103.

7. De Montfort, *True Devotion*, pp. 158–160.

8. Bossuet, p. 63.

9. De Montfort, *True Devotion*, p. 195.

10. Philip of Harveng, *In Cantica Canticorum,* 6, 50, quoted in Gambero, *Mary in the Middle Ages,* p. 180.

11. Eudes, *Admirable Heart*, p. 41.

12. Peter Julian Eymard, quoted in Supple, p. 129.

13. Antonin Gilbert Sertillanges, *Spirituality* (New York: McMullen, 1954), p. 215.

14. John Eudes, quoted in Supple, p. 86.

15. Bonaventure, quoted in Supple, p. 72.

16. Marguerite Tjader Harris, ed., *Birgitta of Sweden: Life and Selected Revelations* (New York: Paulist, 1990), pp. 182–183, 185.

17. R.P. Léonce de Grandmaison, "Prayer for the Heart of a Child," quoted in Father Mark, "The Joy of Letting Go," http://vultus. stblogs.org.

Chapter Twelve. The Holy Name of Mary: Doing What the Angels Do

1. Thomas Aquinas, quoted in Supple, p. 8.
2. Jean Gerson, quoted in Gambero, *Mary in the Middle Ages*, pp. 283–284.
3. John Eudes, *Meditations on Various Subjects* (New York: P.J. Kenedy & Sons, 1947), pp. 205–206.
4. De Montfort, *The Secret of Mary*, in *God Alone*, p. 369.
5. Peter Canisius, quoted in Supple, p. 9.
6. De Montfort, *The Secret of Mary*, in *God Alone*, pp. 369, 370.
7. William of Saint-Thierry, "He Loved Us First," excerpt from *On the Contemplation of God*, used in the Roman Office of Readings for Monday of the Third Week in Advent and reprinted at www.crossroadsinitiative.com.
8. Henry Suso, quoted in Supple, p. 8.
9. Benedict XVI, *On the Way to Jesus Christ* (San Francisco: Ignatius, 2005), p. 31.
10. William McLoughlin and Jill Pinnock, *Mary for Time and Eternity: Papers on Mary and Ecumenism* (Herefordshire, England: Gracewing, 2007), p. 69.
11. Richard of St. Lawrence, quoted at www.holywoundsapostolate.com.
12. Ephrem the Syrian, quoted in Supple, p. 6.
13. Ambrose, quoted in Supple, p. 6.
14. Thomas à Kempis, quoted at www.holywoundsapostolate.com.
15. Bonaventure, quoted in Supple, p. 7.
16. De Montfort, *God Alone*, pp. 292–293.
17. Words of the Blessed Virgin to St. Bridget, quoted at www.holywoundsapostolate.com.
18. Bonaventure, quoted in Supple, p. 7.
19. The words of the Blessed Virgin to St. Bridget, quoted at www.holywoundsapostolate.com.
20. Thomas à Kempis, quoted in Rama Coomaraswamy, ed., *Invocation of the Name of Jesus* (Louisville: Fons Vitae, 1999), pp. 155–156.
21. Alphonsus Liguori, quoted at www.holywoundsapostolate.com.

22. Bonaventure, quoted at www.holywoundsapostolate.com.

23. De Montfort, *God Alone*, pp. 369, 370; *True Devotion*, pp. 120–121.

24. Bl. Raymond Jordano, quoted at www.holywoundsapostolate.com.

25. Eadmer of Canterbury, quoted in Gambero, *Mary in the Middle Ages*, pp. 121, 122.

26. Jacques Fesch, *Light Over the Scaffold, Prison Letters of Jacques Fesch, and Cell 18, Unedited Letters of Jacques Fesch,* ed. Augustin Michel Lemonnier (Staten Island, N.Y.: Alba House, 2001), p. 99.

27. Fesch, pp. 98–99.

28. Bernard, quoted in Gambero, *Mary in the Middle Ages*, p. 140.

29. De Montfort, *God Alone*, pp. 292–293.

30. De Montfort, *God Alone*, pp. 292–293.

31. Henry Suso, quoted in Supple, p. 8.

CHAPTER THIRTEEN. OUR LADY OF THE ROSARY: CONTEMPLATING WITH MARY THE FACE OF CHRIST

1. De Montfort, *The Secret of the Rosary*, Second Rose, in *God Alone*, pp. 157–158.

2. See Benedict XVI, *Deus Caritas Est*, no. 1.

3. John Paul II, *Redemptor Hominis*, March 4, 1979, no. 10, www.vatican.va.

4. Columba Marmion, *Christ, the Life of the Soul* (Bethesda, Md.: Zaccheus, 2005), p. 28.

5. Romano Guardini, *The Rosary of Our Lady,* trans. H. von Schuecking (Manchester, N.H.: Sophia Institute, 1983), pp. 37, 38, 39–40.

6. Hans Urs von Balthasar, *Mary for Today* (San Francisco: Ignatius, 1988), pp. 43–44.

CHAPTER FOURTEEN. OUR LADY OF GUADALUPE: THE ARRIVAL OF THE SIGN OF NEW LIFE

1. Eduardo Chavez, *Our Lady of Guadalupe and St. Juan Diego: The Historical Evidence*, trans. Carmen Tevino and Veronica Montano (Lanham, Md.: Rowman & Littlefield, 2006), p. 12.

2. Louis Lavelle, quoted in Pierre-Marie Emonet, *The Greatest Marvel of Nature: An Introduction to the Philosophy of the Human Person*, trans. Robert R. Barr (New York: Crossroad, 2000), p. 67.

3. Joseph Vidal de Figueroa, quoted in Francisco Raymond Schulte, *Mexican Spirituality: Its Sources and Mission in the Earliest Guadalupan Sermons* (Lanham, Md.: Rowman & Littlefield, 2002), pp. 96, 97.

4. Vidal de Figueroa, quoted in Schulte, pp. 78–79.

5. Luis de Santa Theresa, quoted in Schulte, pp. 79, 81.

6. Antonio Lopez Murto, quoted in Schulte, pp. 81, 84.

7. Francis Johnston, *The Wonder of Guadalupe: The Origin and Cult of the Miraculous Image of the Blessed Virgin in Mexico* (Charlotte, N.C.: TAN, 1981), inside front cover.

8. Eduardo Chavez, "In the Hands of Our Merciful Mother," *Columbia*, vol. 89, no. 3 (March 2009), p. 24.

9. Francisco de Fuentes y Carrion, quoted in Schulte, p. 127.

10. Johnston, p. 118.

11. Schulte, p. 129.

12. Juan de Villa y Sanchez, quoted in Schulte, pp. 85–86.

13. Chavez, *Our Lady of Guadalupe*, pp. 140–141.

14. Quoted in Johnston, p. 53.

CHAPTER FIFTEEN. THE SATURDAY MEMORIAL OF THE BLESSED VIRGIN MARY: EMBRACING MARY'S MEMORY

1. Vatican Congregation for Divine Worship, Directory on Popular Piety and the Liturgy, no. 188, quoting from the Congregation for Divine Worship Circular Letter *Guidelines and Proposals for the Celebration of the Marian Year*, 2002, no. 5, www.vatican.va.

2. Benedict XVI, *Jesus of Nazareth: From the Baptism in the Jordan to the Transfiguration*, trans. Adrian J. Walker (San Francisco: Ignatius, 2007), p. 234.

3. Benedict XVI, *Deus Caritas Est*, no. 1.

4. Benedict XVI, *Jesus of Nazareth*, pp. 231, 232.

5. Benedict XVI, *Jesus of Nazareth*, p. 234.

6. Benedict XVI, *Jesus of Nazareth*, p. 233.

select bibliography

Amadeus of Lausanne. *Eight Homilies on the Praises of Blessed Mary.* Kalamazoo, Mich.: Cistercian, 1979.

Benedict XVI (Joseph Ratzinger). *Jesus of Nazareth: From the Baptism in the Jordan to the Transfiguration,* trans. Adrian J. Walker. San Francisco: Ignatius, 2007.

Bernard of Clairvaux. *Homilies in Praise of the Blessed Virgin Mary.* Kalamazoo, Mich.: Cistercian, 1993.

Bossuet, Jacques-Bénigne. *Devotion to the Blessed Virgin: Being the Substance of All the Sermons for Mary's Feasts Throughout the Year.* London: Longmans, Green, 1899.

Cessario, Romanus. *Perpetual Angelus: As the Saints Pray the Rosary.* New York: Alba House, 1995.

Chavez, Eduardo. *Our Lady of Guadalupe and St. Juan Diego: The Historical Evidence.* Lanham, Md.: Rowman & Littlefield, 2006.

Daley, Brian E., trans. *On the Dormition of Mary: Early Patristic Homilies.* Crestwood, N.Y.: St. Vladimir's Seminary Press, 1998.

De Montfort, Louis-Marie. *God Alone: The Collected Writings of St. Louis Marie de Montfort.* Bay Shore, N.Y.: Montfort, 1995.

————. *True Devotion to the Blessed Virgin.* Trans. Malachy Gerard Carroll. Langley Bucks, England: Society of Saint Paul, 1962.

Eudes, John. *The Admirable Heart of Mary.* New York: P.J. Kenedy & Sons, 1948.

Gambero, Luigi. *Mary and the Fathers of the Church: The Blessed Virgin Mary in Patristic Thought.* San Francisco: Ignatius, 1999.

————. *Mary in the Middle Ages: The Blessed Virgin Mary in the Thought of Medieval Latin Theologians.* San Francisco: Ignatius, 2005.

Gregory Palamas. *Mary the Mother of God: Sermons by St. Gregory Palamas.* South Canaan, Pa.: Mount Thabor, 2005.

Hobbs, Richard. *Fifteen Mysteries in the Life of Jesus.* Staten Island, N.Y.: Alba House, 2002.

Jacob of Serug. *On the Mother of God.* Crestwood, N.Y.: St. Vladimir's Seminary Press, 1998.

John Paul II. *Redemptoris Mater: Encyclical Letter on the Blessed Virgin Mary in the Life of the Pilgrim Church.* Vatican: Libreria Editrice Vaticana, 1987.

————. *Rosarium Virginis Mariae: Apostolic Letter on the Most Holy Rosary.* Vatican: Libreria Editrice Vaticana, 2002.

————. *Theotokos: Woman, Mother, Disciple: A Catechesis on Mary, Mother of God.* Boston: Pauline, 2000.

Johnston, Francis. *The Wonder of Guadalupe: The Origin and Cult of the Miraculous Image of the Blessed Virgin Mary.* Charlotte, N.C.: TAN, 1981.

Noe, Virgilio, ed. *Prayers to Mary.* New York: Catholic Book, 1987.

Rahner, Hugo. *Our Lady and the Church.* Bethesda, Md.: Zaccheus, 2004.

Rilke, Rainer Maria. *The Life of the Virgin Mary: A Cycle of Poems.* Trans. Christine McNeill. Dublin: Dedalus, 2003.

Schulte, Francisco Raymond. *Mexican Spirituality: Its Sources and Mission in the Earliest Guadalupan Sermons.* Lanham, Md.: Rowman & Littlefield, 2002.

Stravinskas, Peter, ed. *The Catholic Answer Book of Mary.* Huntington, Ind.: Our Sunday Visitor, 2000.

Supple, David, ed. *Virgin Wholly Marvelous: Praises of Our Lady by the Popes, Councils, St.s, and Doctors of the Church.* Cambridge, Mass.: Ravengate, 1981.

About the Author

Father Peter John Cameron, O.P., is founding editor-in-chief of the monthly worship aid *Magnificat*. He is also a teacher of preaching and director of Blackfriars Repertory Theatre in New York City. His other books include *The Classics of Catholic Spirituality*, the three-volume *To Praise, To Bless, To Preach: Spiritual Reflections on the Sunday Gospels*, *Why Preach: Encountering Christ in God's Word*, and *Jesus, Present Before Me: Meditations for Eucharistic Adoration*.